AN APOLOGY
FOR THE ARTS

BY

W. MACNEILE DIXON

LONDON

EDWARD ARNOLD & CO.

Copyright

First Published 1944

Printed in Great Britain by
Butler & Tanner Ltd., Frome and London

Contents

Foreword

For some years before the era of our present troubles I entertained myself with the idea of devoting a quiet retirement to the writing of a slight book upon a great subject, no less than the place and significance of the arts in human life. They possess a secret worth the probing. They have a peculiar and singular attraction. They have been venerated above all other human achievements. The Greeks, a discerning folk, provided them with a divine patronage—the Muses. The masters in the arts are the remembered ones, the best beloved and most honoured among the immortals. Why it has been so, why it should be so, seemed to me an enquiry not merely of interest but of some importance.

The hoped-for day of leisure arrived, accompanied however by the storm of war, and my project, like a million million others, perished in the flames of the devouring conflagration still raging. My own house was wrecked, my books and possessions hastily consigned to some pony stables near Oxford. There, in their unnatural surroundings, they still are, and the house remains uninhabitable. In the course of the desperate affair upon which we are engaged, in the midst of the tremendous events of our times, these hardships are not, indeed, worth the mention. The book I contemplated will never be written, but that too is no more than a bagatelle. The future will provide better books by better minds. For until thinking itself be abandoned, philosophers, great and small, will find in the affection of mankind for poetry, painting, music and the other arts a passion inviting their closest attention.

How surprising its presence, how serene the passage of that star—the love of loveliness—through the cloudy and tempestuous heavens of human history. It argues, does it not? something positive, something ethereal in man's nature, clearly in need of elucidation. And more especially in these days when the great Battle of the Values is at its height, when science is in the ascendant, and the arts in adversity, when men, anxious-eyed, look around them for an answer to the question of questions, 'what matters most in the ordering of this our brief terrestrial existence,' it appears to me eminently appropriate on the very threshold of that grand enquiry to ask ourselves, as did Kant, what rank and authority can justly be claimed for, or assigned to, the imaginative or creative faculty of the human mind among its neighbouring powers and faculties in our intellectual armoury ? Is this rank and authority in any sense of major account, or possibly even in some sense supreme ?

The following discourses have for the most part already appeared in print and might, perhaps, be regarded as surveys or approaches in the foothills preliminary to an attempt upon the ascent of a lofty peak in the distance. For an undertaking so difficult and hazardous I must admit my qualifications to be slender enough. Putting poetry aside—the chief pleasure and consolation of my life—they have however been fostered over many years by visits to a great number, if not most, of the more famous sites, buildings and galleries of Europe, as far apart as Jerusalem and Paris, all of them as exhilarating as they were instructive, and not least the last, a brief holiday spent in Geneva, which offered an opportunity, immediately before the outbreak of this present war, to see some of the choicest works of El Greco, Goya and Velasquez, a revelation in itself of the height, depth and piercing penetration of man's astounding powers, a wonder to behold. They distil for us, the masters in these mysterious arts, an elixir, a healing medicine for the vexations of the soul, like the smile on the noble face of the young Leonardo da Vinci, which it is recorded ' brought refreshment to every downcast spirit.'

Civilization is in these days a word on every lip. What precisely is meant by it is not at all times easy to determine. It is at least my own conviction that for civilization, in any shape or form worthy admiration, the arts are the main pillars or rather the architects and builders. Without them it has never arisen and cannot arise ; without them it cannot and will not stand.

Campbell (1928) and *Thoughts for the Times* (1940) were delivered as lectures before the University of Glasgow ; *Poetry and National Character*, the Leslie Stephen Lecture of 1915, was published by the Cambridge University Press in that year ; *Chatterton* formed the Warton Lecture of the British Academy in 1930 ; *English and Scottish Ballads* was contributed to *The Quarterly Review* (John Murray) in 1898, and *Civilization and the Arts* to the American Magazine, *Fortune*, in 1942. I am indebted to their original sponsors for permission to reprint them here. My grateful thanks are also due to my friends, Professor Dewar of Reading and Miss Maude G. May, for their kind assistance while the following pages were passing through the press.

W. M. D.

Civilization and the Arts

The English poets and men of letters of the seventeenth and eighteenth centuries claimed for themselves a high office. It was no less a claim than to be missionaries of civilization. And what was civilization ? The outcome of an effort, they would have answered, to render human society, in all possible ways open to mankind, less harassing and more agreeable, the effort to soften life's asperities, to substitute persuasion and good sense for the barbaric violence, threatenings, and slaughter by which human intercourse has in the past been so terribly disfigured, to substitute the enlightening exchange of opinions for the destructive exchange of grapeshot. It represented, in brief, simply an attempt, however unconscious, to elevate human life above material needs and preoccupations, to provide it with spiritual interests, to introduce into our short and anxious lives as much of grace and dignity as were attainable in the conditions of man's estate. In this great endeavour—so the Renaissance humanists believed—the arts in general, poetry, music, painting, sculpture, architecture, might not only be of assistance, but, setting religion aside, should prove the most promising and most potent of all available agencies. Conversely, the standard of civilization attained by any race or nation might, they held, be justly estimated by its care for these things, the place they held in the estimation of its citizens.

In a word, art and literature were not merely to be regarded as pursuits pleasant in themselves, as agreeable forms of escape from anxiety and boredom or mere ornamental additions to social intercourse, but beyond doubt the most valuable of all allies in the long battle for a nobler and a better future, as making for the common good of human society. This engaging conception found, it may be conceded, at least a firm basis in the universal interest the pursuit and practice of the arts had through historic times excited, each in its own manner and measure, among the tribes and peoples of mankind. They had everywhere and in all ages been in some fashion cultivated and in some degree enjoyed. They had met, so history seemed to report, certain deep-seated needs of human nature, and—a very relevant and significant circumstance—they had in no respect added to the distresses or tribulations of the race, never been employed as the instruments of tyranny to inflict cruelty, to support injustice, to imprison thought. The practice of these arts had never led to revolutions, massacres, or wars. Could as much be said of politics, or even of religion ? They had done much for the welfare of suffering mortals, so, under Renaissance influences, the humanists, poets, and men of letters contended, might they not be trusted to do much more ?

So simple a faith in the efficacy of art and letters as the most powerful of all civilizing agencies wears in our time a somewhat antiquated air. It has lost not a little of its early charm. Its open advocates are few. We have long since transferred our allegiance to other remedies for our ills. We have put our trust in political, economic, and scientific remedies—yet, judging from the present state of the world, without any very dazzling or resounding success. The benefits conferred upon humanity by modern science are, indeed, beyond enumeration. They call for our wonder and astonishment. And who could fail to take pride in the magnificent witness it bears to the powers and resources of the human mind ? Its victories have been spectacular, its successes border upon the miraculous. For some reason, nevertheless, these victories and successes do not include those for which we hoped. Wiser, no doubt, we are, yet the age of science, which made us so, has proved a disappointment. We, its children, are no happier, perhaps less happy, than our predecessors. How is this ? If it be so, the poets and artists need not in the proud presence of the men of science confess themselves superfluous persons, nor altogether hide their diminished heads.

But there remains in this context a searching question not to be ignored. However they may have served humanity in the youth of the world, is there in an age of reason like our own, which bows the knee in reason's shrine and knows no other deity, any longer need of, or any future for, the arts at all? Is it not the truth, if we can bear to hear it, that their day is done? Absurd, you say. Yet great men have told us so, many men have feared it. ' Thought and reflection,' announced Hegel, in no uncertain voice, ' have taken their flight above fine art.' Macaulay was not less oracular upon the matter. ' As civilization advances,' he declared, ' poetry almost necessarily declines.' Peacock sounded the same confident note. ' When the mind becomes more enlarged and comprehensive, as reason gains the ascendancy over imagination and feeling, the empire of thought is withdrawn from poetry, which can no longer accompany it on its progress, and leaves the understanding to advance alone.' And again, ' Poetry can never make a philospher nor statesman, nor in any class of life a useful or rational man.' Well, it is a fair challenge, and should be met.

What, then, can sensibly be said for the pursuit and practice of these arts? The order of precedence among them—a pretty enough enquiry, if perhaps a trifle contentious—is not at the moment in question, and the word ' poetry ' may fairly be employed as representative of the fine arts in general, with which it is closely associated, with whose outlook upon human life theirs may without demur be identified. Music and painting, sculpture and architecture are all poetry in its widest sense. The nobler arts are a sisterhood, and poetry may be permitted to speak for the rhythmical family to which all belong.

Here, then, is the question. Have we now, in a world no longer young, outgrown poetry, as children outgrow their toys? Does the advance in knowledge toll the death knell, as Hegel predicted, of the fine arts? Is it in sober fact possible to be so wise, so well informed, as to have little or no further need of them? Are the great poets and artists of the world—

assuming the comparison not wholly senseless—less trustworthy as leaders of thought, as interpreters of the universe to their fellow creatures, or of ourselves to ourselves, than the thinkers in other fields ? Are they of less consequence or of lower intellectual stature than the followers of pure reason, the men of science and the philosophers ?

It is commonly assumed or believed that the arts deal in fancies rather than in facts, in flights of imagination rather than hard realities, that poetry is 'a kind of ingenious nonsense,' that one and all they are the occupations of idle dreamers, and that we must take counsel with men of stiffer grain, of a very different and superior order to assist us in the building of a better world. Well is it so ?

We cannot fail to observe that poets and artists are seldom included in the accredited histories of human thought. They are not usually mentioned among the profound and penetrating philosophic minds. And yet I cannot avoid asking myself, what else, if not thinking, was Cervantes doing when he wrote that wonder of wonders among books, *Don Quixote*, or Ictinus when he designed that miracle of loveliness, the Parthenon at Athens ? For my part I cannot assign, let us say Euripides, to a lower intellectual rank than Hobbes or Locke, declare Beethoven less logical than Kant, or Rembrandt than John Stuart Mill. To think Michelangelo's mind less profound than Galileo's, Shakespeare's less subtle than Spinoza's, seems to me a strange reversal of the truth. For the poets and artists had a talent hard to match. To their mental depth and acuteness they added an imaginative, a creative power so rare and astonishing as, on that count alone, to win the hearts of men. Comparisons are odious, and in this field also a trifle ridiculous. If made at all, it must peremptorily be said that to succeed greatly in the arts demands not less 'fundamental brainwork' than in any of the higher undertakings of the mind. Within the field of pure reason and intelligence the poets and artists take, in their own manner, and by no means in an inferior manner, their rightful place with the most exact and comprehensive thinkers the world has known.

No one in his senses will attempt to diminish the glory of modern science. Let us, however, bear in mind an obvious truth. Before so much as the word ' science ' rose above the intellectual horizon, countless millions of human beings had passed across the great stage, lived in most respects much as we ourselves live, as perforce all must live, eating and drinking, marrying, sorrowing, rejoicing. Despite all our advantages, all our knowledge, in their day and generation it does not appear they were less happy and contented than we. The Greeks, in their most brilliant era, who attained two thousand years ago so high a pitch of culture, knew nothing of science in our understanding of it, its conveniences and blessings. Of chemistry, of astronomy, and all the rest they had not a modern schoolboy's knowledge. Physiology and pathology did not exist. Medicine and surgery were in their babyhood. Nevertheless in their absence, even in the absence of the wonderful modern inventions, Plato and Aristotle, Aeschylus and Aristophanes, Socrates and Pericles appear to have suffered little hardship, to have thought and written, carved and built as well, to say the least of it, as most men since, and in the absence of all the paraphernalia of modern education to have attained a highly respectable degree of wisdom and civility. How are we to suppose all this came about ? One wonders occasionally whether our much talked-of civilization has all the advantages our fancy paints, whether its accumulated machinery of fast and furious distractions leaves us time for thought at all, or bears any profitable relation to our inner lives.

To what conclusions, then, are we driven ? Not, indeed, that the things our forerunners lacked are worthless things—the railways, the telephones, the electric light have their value. Conclude we must, however, that a high state of civilization, define it as you will, may be attained without them. It does not consist, as some have fondly imagined, in the knowledge of nature's laws or the control of her forces. And to another inference no less certain and important : machinery cannot make a civilization. If we propose to look to science for our salvation, there is this to bear in mind. Science moves on the circumference of our lives. She has her being in the outer and physical world, as far removed from the interior region of our deepest and most intimate experiences as the northern from the southern pole.

There is, as everyone knows, a province of human life—and only upon reflection do we perceive how vast, how boundless is that province—to whose interests and problems the most extensive knowledge or control of nature's machinery affords no entrance, a country upon which the bright sun of science sheds not a ray of light. It is the country of the soul. We have our affections and sympathies, we have loves and friendships, we have hopes and fears and admirations, inmates of a province of real things as broad and deep as the telescopic heavens above our heads. Of these things science never speaks. She sits above the battle and has no share in our joys and sorrows. Of good and evil, freedom and justice, science has nothing to say. The scientific vocabulary does not include such words as beauty or heroism, nobility or charm, resignation or despair, kindness or generosity, character or conduct. Not until you ponder such words do you perceive how narrow and inhuman is the view that omits them, the internal experiences with which our minds are so continuously occupied from the cradle to the grave.

Is it necessary to remind ourselves that the physical sciences exclude the humanities, and are not interested in the great pageant of the world, the rise and fall of kingdoms, the lives of great men, statesmen, martyrs, soldiers, saints, or their part in the shaping of human history, that they never so much as mention the revolutions, the wars, the religions, the mighty events in the panorama of the past ? How vast, then, is the gap in the scientific programme. And how fantastic to suppose, if we do suppose, that the sciences, which are by their nature excluded or exclude themselves from the province of the heart and its affections, can minister to our most urgent and deepest necessities, and, unassisted, build for us the society of our dreams. The arts, which are at home where the sciences are strangers, in the very region where logic is at a loss and the most lofty understanding ill at ease, can hardly fail to prove themselves the better guides and interpreters through the labyrinth of mankind's perplexities.

Ours is an age of crowding doubts, and among them a deep misgiving haunts the world to-day. It has begun to doubt the power or sufficiency of the unassisted reason to resolve its torturing problems, and of political and economic devices to meet and serve its needs. Pursued though it be through weary days and sleepless nights, the search for material remedies to soothe or cure our spiritual distresses can have only one end— failure. Much more will be needed than to feed the hungry, house the poor, clothe the destitute, however generously contrived and devotedly administered these undertakings may be. The day of acceptance of the great truth approaches, than which a greater was never yet proclaimed, that ' man does not live by bread alone.' With its acceptance and not till then will be laid the foundation stone of a civilization worthy the name.

Four hundred years have passed since that famous era of startling events and discoveries entitled by historians the Renaissance. We are still governed by Renaissance ways of thought, and among the heart-shaking, spirit-searching thoughts that took shape in the fourteenth and fifteenth centuries, and then entered and took possession of the European mind, one new idea must be assigned pride of place, so commanding was it, so uplifting, so supreme. It was the idea of progress. The idea of a continuous, never-ending advance of the human race towards a nobler and a happier world, an earthly paradise. The very thought aroused hope and stimulated effort. It provided an aim, an ideal, an adventure, a common undertaking for all mankind. This immense expectation or inspired vision, to us so familiar and so natural, had, difficult as it is to believe, never entered and had no place in the mental furniture of the mediæval nor yet the ancient world. The men of earlier days entertained no such hope for themselves or the generations to come. No such sunlit, encouraging prospect had ever before been harboured on earth since creation's dawn. What wonder, then, that a conception that magnificently widened the hopes and enhanced the values of life captured the human mind? For it transformed the whole scene of existence.

How, then, do matters stand to-day? The Renaissance had two sides. It displayed itself in an enthusiasm for the newly discovered classical civilization in its brilliant achievements; it displayed itself also in the spirit of scientific enquiry. To which, if any comparison can be instituted between them, do we owe the most; from which may we expect in the future the greatest benefits? So far scientific enquiry is in the saddle and leads the field. Yet is it not evident that for some reason, since our attention has been mainly directed to the external world and material things and our knowledge of them so marvellously increased, the human spirit has suffered hardship and become of less account, human life diminished in importance, and our hearts have been depressed? Can it be truly said that during the reign of science, during the centuries of its triumphant progress, we have attained a higher standard of humanity, justice, honour, or chivalry? Is there to be found around us to-day an increase of happiness, any clear or certain evidence of higher and more hopeful spirits? Has brute force disappeared or given way in any degree to reasonableness or courtesy? Can we assert that truth, beauty and nobility are held in greater respect than in earlier days, or that in our needs and requirements there has been any spiritual progress? If science, then, has not carried the banner of progress to the heights we hoped to climb, the causes of our discontent are not far to seek. We asked her to perform an impossible task to which she never addressed herself, and with which she was not concerned. In her own and chosen undertaking, the study of nature and of our material surroundings, the successes of science have surpassed all expectation. The failure was not hers but ours. It was a cardinal error to assume that she could make any substantial contribution to the improvement of human nature, or to the elevation and refinement of human character or human conduct. Intoxicated by the conquests of physical nature, we supposed them sufficient for all our needs, and in our exultation forgot the simple truth that man is not merely a reasoning being, that knowledge of nature's ways does not satisfy his heart, nor does a purely intellectual diet feed his moral and spiritual being, his ideals, aims, and aspirations.

You recall Pope's famous line, ' The proper study of mankind is man.' And we may, I think, at least agree that in the interests of any form of civilization yet devised the conquest of man over himself, over his will and passions, over his animal nature, is of no less importance than the subjugation and control of the forces of nature.

If any subject occupies the public mind to-day it is education. But what kind of education have we in view ? To educate the mind is difficult enough, but how much more troublesome the education of the emotions. Accuracy of thinking is not, as is commonly supposed, a rarer thing than refinement or delicacy of sensibility. In my belief it is much more widely distributed and more highly appreciated. Far more care is given by the state to the education of the intellect than of the feelings. The values of quick wits, a good memory, sharp intelligence, and exact thinking are universally recognized. But where are we to look for a similar recognition of the values of right feeling, of taste, of delicate discernment, of quality rather than force of mind, of sensitivity and sympathy in social intercourse, which are powers and faculties of the soul ? By his taste we distinguish the scholar from the pedant, by his possession of taste, the gentleman from the barbarian. It is the standard of refinement prevailing among its citizens that exalts a nation, and by which a civilization may be judged. Brains and knowledge you may have in abundance and yet remain a savage. Examples are not far to seek in the world to-day. Look around and you will, I think, become vividly aware that to educate and discipline the soul is of no less vital consequence in any society than to accumulate information or add a cubit to its intellectual stature.

Suppose we were to give our thoughts another turn. 'After all,' remarked a Cambridge mathematician of *Paradise Lost*, 'what does it prove?' And clearly, if exact knowledge or power over nature's forces be your aim, poetry, music, and the other arts will not hasten to your aid. If you are asked of the frieze of the Parthenon, or a melody of Handel's, or one of Turner's landscapes, 'What does it prove?' you have to confess that it proves nothing. Not one of these or similar works demonstrates any proposition or leads to any conclusion of which you can make any obvious or profitable use. The fine arts labour under this awkward disability. They have little connection with the multitudinous activities or undertakings of the community. Yet if the pursuit of the arts does nothing more than bring or confer happiness upon the human family, we cannot go far wrong in their company, for in the word 'happiness' is summed up all the desires, all the needs of mankind, yes, even of angels, or the gods themselves.

That brilliant Irishman, Richard Steele, lost an estate by his choice of a party. But he preferred, he said, the state of his mind to the state of his fortune. The fine arts prove nothing. To speak of them in connection with our social problems seems utterly irrelevant. Statesmen pay small attention to them. One hears no mention of them at elections. Politely accepted they may be, and allowed to be ornamental, none the less also tacitly assumed to be of small consequence. The urgent question arises whether a man's state of mind or a people's state of mind is in fact of minor or trifling importance, or on the contrary, as Steele perceived, of major and transcendent importance. What can be more useful than a state of mind? It is the most useful of all things, an end in itself. For a happy state of mind is a heavenly state of mind, and takes you back to the Garden of Eden before the Fall, before the desire for knowledge brought about the great catastrophe.

To claim the poets, painters, musicians as the best friends and allies of civilization may very well be regarded by the majority of men as a mere extravagance, a high and mighty claim, not to be seriously entertained. The answer is, a still more exalted claim has been advanced for them. Let me recall to you the attitude of that remarkable genius, painter, poet, citizen of London, William Blake, towards the fine arts. Blake went much further than his eighteenth-century predecessors in respect for their efficacy as missionaries of civilization. He advanced a singular doctrine. They were, he held, the truest interpreters and representatives of Christianity itself. Nor was this opinion set forth by Blake in any vague or nebulous fashion, but with the most intense conviction of its truth, in the most distinct, forthright, and astonishing language. He identified Christianity with the love and practice of the fine arts. Not only did he assert categorically that Christianity is art and art Christianity; not only did he say 'Jesus and the Apostles were all artists,' that 'Prayer is the study of art, Praise is the practice of art'; not only did he proclaim that the three sons of Noah, who survived the Flood, were to be symbolically understood as Poetry, Painting, and Music: he went so far as to make the somewhat alarming declaration, 'A poet, a painter, a musician, an architect, the man or woman who is not one of these is not a Christian.' When you have taken breath and pondered these remarks, you may conclude them symptoms of evident lunacy, nothing more than the excursions of an un-balanced mind, a mere froth of wild words. It would be, I think, much too rash and hasty a judgment. The world at large is not interested in ordinary men who go the way it goes, however successfully. It is interested in men who go their own way, artists, poets, dreamers, who are without common sense, but have some kind of uncommon sense, which startles and kindles the mind of the observer, men who stumble and fall when they walk, but at moments attain the miracle of flight. 'There is something in the madness of this man,' said Wordsworth of William Blake, 'which interests me more than the sanity of Lord Byron and Walter Scott.' 'This man,' wrote Swinburne, 'had never lived in the low places of thought.' Verdicts like these give us pause.

What, then, was Blake's meaning and contention? His doctrine, however extravagantly expressed, is easily comprehended. The fine arts are essentially religious, and for this reason : they interpret the world and human life in the language of the soul, as distinguished from reason and science, which attempt to interpret them exclusively in terms of the intellect. To the assumption that reason is the only avenue to truth Blake opposed an inflexible and unyielding front, as did Pascal when he wrote, 'The heart has its reasons of which reason knows nothing.' Blake believed with passionate conviction that man's reason, enslaved in the service of his bodily necessities, is lost and cannot but be lost when it attempts to enter the realm of supersensuous reality, the region of ultimate and innermost truth, when it presumptuously proposes to unveil the last secrets of the universe. It is lost as hopelessly as the geologist or mathematician is lost in the inner and spiritual realms. What has physics or chemistry to say of our ideals and sympathies, our hopes and fears and longings ? Are there no such things ; are these words without meaning ?

When you rule out all evidence save the evidence of material things, supplied by the five bodily senses, 'The universe belies you and your heart refutes a hundred times the mind's conceit.' In this matter Blake was disturbed by no doubts, no hesitations. As when, for example, he said of Flaxman's death, 'I cannot think of death as more than the going out of one room into another.' Refusing to accept a mechanical universe, mere physical phenomena, as the final truth, the reality of all realities, he held a very different creed. Poetry, painting, music disclosed, as religion also discovered, a depth and mystery in the world beyond all physical investigation, and were in consequence at one with Christianity upon the great and paramount issues. They should be regarded as windows into the transcendental world, invisible to mortal sight, presenting wider prospects, a vision of beauty in closest correspondence with the aspirations and affections of mankind. They were, in William Blake's own charming phrase, 'three powers in man of conversing with Paradise.'

Such then, in briefest outline, is Blake's doctrine. Can it be accepted? It assigns to the aspirations and intimations of our innermost being a higher authority than the authority of the intellect. They penetrate, it asserts, more deeply, into the true heart of the universe than the logical understanding, they bring with them 'authentic tidings of invisible things.' This philosophy runs counter—let us be clear on the matter—to the strongest tides of modern thought. The world, however, is not yet at an end, and there are centuries yet to come. We must expect as many and amazing alterations of thought in the future as the past has ever seen.

We approach now the main issue. To the arts has been assigned an exalted rank above all other undertakings, a peculiar respect, reverence, authority. They appear to have their natural home in a region impenetrable by reason. They point to a world above our heads, a transcendental world, in which, if anywhere, we may hope to find the fulfilment of our heart's desire. Does such a world exist, or is it a mirage, a lying vision only? Here is the great divide, the momentous parting of the ways in human thought. Here every man must make his choice. Here on one side stand the rationalists, men who decline, like St. Thomas, to advance beyond the evidence of the senses, to believe until they have seen with their eyes, touched, and handled, the men who put their trust in the human intellect, its findings and no other. And here in opposition are the men of religion, the poets and artists who place their trust in the inner vision, the intimations of the soul and its affections.

And not only the men of religion and the poets. Listen to Nietzsche, that hard, disillusioned thinker. 'There is in all great art an enigmatic profundity, an infinity of background.' And again : 'The man of philosophic turn has a foreboding that beneath this reality in which we live and move and have our being another and altogether different reality lies concealed.' Yes, they have a foreboding not easily exorcised. Keep company with the arts and it will continue to haunt you. They have apparently nothing more than a decorative value and none the less possess a supreme value. They appear to be concerned with matters of no great consequence, and yet, it seems, introduce you to matters of vital consequence. Keep company with them, and without warning, reading a poem, listening to a piece of music, looking at a picture, you may be entangled, as Nietzsche says, in the infinities. One never knows when the heavens may open, and in the shock of this bewilderment, face to face with the immeasurable universe, a man looks about him with new awareness, new apprehension. It is then that suddenly the whole scene of existence is perceived in its overwhelming immensity, its true dimensions. What may it or may it not contain ? It is then that the values of the fleeting world are weighed in the balance. Even the plain man is exposed to this strange peril. He finds an inexplicable fascination in these enigmatic arts. He may not take them seriously. Yet some secret sympathy, some inborn loyalty draws him, do what he will, to admire, to listen, and to gaze. So at any moment he may be swept away into the deep sea and cannot but enquire, 'What means all this ?'

When you enter the temple of the arts you enter a building dedicated to the Muses, and the soul is there disturbed by a sense of how great and terrible, how strange and beautiful is this universe of ours. Make human life as trivial as you please, there remains the simple, positive, undeniable fact among the other facts—the eating and drinking, walking and talking—that we are taking part in cosmic affairs, of a magnitude beyond all imagination to compass or language to express. All finite things have their roots in the infinite and if you wish to understand life at all, you cannot tear it out of its context. And that context, astounding even to bodily eyes, is the heaven of stars and the incredible procession of the great galaxies.

In poetry, like its sister arts, you discern—it is common knowledge—not only a peculiar aloofness from life's daily routine, but a singular language. By this idiom the arts are known, the form and grace, the celestial quality, the rhythm of their speech. And what is rhythm, and why celestial? Celestial since, however it be defined, it is, in fact, the speech of nature and of life. Unseen and unobserved it rules the movements of the heavens, guides the atom and the star, swings the seasons and the days and nights. It illuminates the world in the passage of light, controls the winds and waves, all the organic processes of our bodies, the sleeping and waking, the pulsing of the heart and lungs. The laws of rhythm are the laws that guide the whole fabric of creation, a structure harmonious in all its manifestations, the smallest as the greatest. To this voice from the depths, this music of the spheres, the soul, the organ of feeling, as distinguished from the understanding, is attuned. There is, as Aristotle's pregnant sentence expresses it ' a kind of relationship between the soul and harmonies and rhythms.' All art is tuneful—not music only. A painting, a statue, a building, each in its own manner, is a melodious creation. Have you observed that a tune has a secret virtue, unique and all its own ? It is a work of magic. It possesses occult properties. When a tune falls on your ear you respond with instant sympathy. You accept without question the suggested measure, you surrender with what Schopenhauer described as ' blind consent ' to its enchantment, its peculiar spell. You cannot deny, argue with, or contradict a tune. You cannot take another point of view or advance a contrary proposition. The tune is your master, you its spellbound servant. And in the arts this peculiar language is everywhere and by all men understood. It is the soul's native tongue, and needs no learning.

There is such a thing as an art of life. Civilization may be described as itself a work of art. As in a Gothic minster you have a great building, the work not of one but many minds and hands, so civilization is a work of communal art, which includes and is indebted to them all. It is a piece of racial architecture, a realization, in its law and order, its etiquette of customs and behaviour, its institutions and ceremonials, of a people's tastes and preferences. It may with truth be regarded as an application to political and civic life, to social intercourse, of the distinction and beauty that delight us in music and poetry. For if beautiful behaviour be not good behaviour, it is something very like it. 'In a thoroughly humanized society,' wrote Santayana, ' everything—clothes, speech, manners, government —is a work of art.' One might, indeed, call its civilization the speaking image of the entire community. In such a society every citizen is himself an artist, and has his share of responsibility as one of its architects.

So far from agreeing with Hegel that ' thought and reflection have taken their flight above fine art,' we must submit that, philosopher though he was, he had not attained so much as a glimmering recognition of its true character, or of its transcendent importance in human life. For art is not merely irreplaceable by any other agency. We can with confidence declare that to the arts, which may well be called divine, belongs a glorious privilege. They have made of beauty a guiding star. They have led mankind on the greatest of all its undertakings and supported it through all the wintry seasons of history. To them we owe the great unwritten principles, the immortal laws that have shaped and guided the conscience of the race. Had

Blake been asked, ' Should we be any worse off if these arts
were to take wings and forsake this planet altogether ? ' he would
have answered, ' Deny humanity their guidance, and you stab
it to the heart. You deprive it of all the spiritual interests,
you drive it back into the aboriginal abyss, a naked animal,
bereft of all its hard-won ethical conceptions, as of justice and
equity, of honour and humanity, of law and magnanimity and
duty.' How right was Tolstoy when he said : ' Art is a great
matter, and its task is enormous.'

No one will deny that modern societies, the whole world
over, are dominated by cupidity, by greed for possession, for
wealth and power. And, as far as I can see, there is no sure
shield against the tyranny of this ruinous passion for possession
save a transference of our affections, if this be possible, from
possession to admiration, from immoderate craving for wealth
and power to an intense longing for beauty and excellence.
Must we for ever continue to think in terms of profit and loss,
of all life's lower and lesser interests ? As the Greeks knew,
' The beautiful is hard, hard to judge, hard to win, hard to
keep.' Yet the love of beauty exists, an ineradicable passion
in every human heart, together with a marvellous capacity for
its appreciation. Whatever else be given us, without beauty we
can never be at peace or at rest. In all forms of beauty, mankind will never cease to take delight till the world ends. Nor
can better testimony to the significance and worth of the gentle
and healing arts be offered than this, that the works of the great
masters never grow old. How reluctant is mankind to part
from them !

The centuries pass, the generations come and go, but in each
there springs up once more a passion for the past and all its
lovely creations. Though we are gone, Persephone will still
gather her flowers in Sicilian Enna, Faust will brood eternally
among his books, Hamlet will never cease to ponder the
mysteries on the battlements of Elsinore.

Poetry and National Character

'There are times,' wrote Leslie Stephen, ' when we feel that we would rather have the actual sounds, the downright utterance of an agonized human being than the far away echo of passion set up in the artistic brain. . . . We tire of the skilfully prepared sentiment, the pretty fancies, the unreal imaginations, and long for the harsh, crude, substantial fact, the actual utterance of men struggling in the dire grasp of unmitigated realities.' Such a desire would be satisfied to-day, for we stand in the grasp of these realities ; and perhaps nothing is, perhaps nothing should be further from our thoughts than matters of literature and art, ' the pretty fancies, the unreal imaginations.' Our ' forward youth,' as in Marvell's Ode, have at their country's call forsaken the ' Muses dear,' and left the ' books in dust ' to ' oil the unused armour's rust.' How faint and faded appear the old academic interests, how unwillingly we concern ourselves with the shadows of the imagined past while our living countrymen challenge by their deeds the heroic records of their forefathers. Happy, indeed, we dare not call these times, yet many a poet, no doubt, many a romancer to come, will celebrate them, it may be with that touch of regret that accompanies the chronicle of famous days, the inevitable touch of regret that they are gone. Happier, they may say, those who had a share in the deeds, happier they may even call us, who are warmed by their generous contagion, than our successors born too late to do more than recall and glorify them.

Yet here at Cambridge, although a university so famous in science as to be almost unconscious of its indisputable supremacy in poetry, here one may at any time speak of poetry openly and without apology. Here too, if anywhere, one may appropriately enquire what light our knowledge of English national character throws upon English poetry, or our knowledge of the poetry upon the national character. Such an enquiry aims, indeed, at no final or scientific truth, a mere 'sally of the mind' it can only support itself upon the tide of its own interest, but at least it proceeds from a fixed point. However far apart or incompatible they may at times appear some connexion between a nation's character and its poetry there must be.

Imagine for a moment an intelligent foreigner—the witness so readily summoned in such investigations—fairly acquainted with a thousand years of our history, the political and commercial activities of the English race, its religious movements, its wars and colonial enterprises, acquainted with all this but unacquainted with our literature. Would he in turning his attention to that literature instinctively expect it to be supreme in poetry, would he anticipate meeting Shakespeare ? Or again, would he find more of the England he had already studied, its essential spirit and genius, in *Beowulf*, in Chaucer, or in Pope ? In his search for that spirit may one not fancy him puzzled by the variety in our poetic moods, by finding Marlowe of the same race as Cowper, or Dryden as Shelley ? All are Englishmen, but would they appear to have anything save their language in common ? Whatever the fundamental qualities of a race may be, and they are neither easily discovered nor stated, such a student could hardly, I fancy, deny that we were a practical and at the same time a poetical folk, or, if not poetical in grain, at least successful in the production of remarkable poetry, a pleasant inconsistency. Possibly he might express surprise at such poetic fertility in an unexpected quarter, in a people obviously of a practical but not obviously of a poetic temper. Certainly he would not ascribe this success to a widely diffused or exceptional artistic sense. Of hideous practicality, of wintry utilitarianism we have often been accused, but no one has ever yet described the Englishman as a born artist. His amiable tolerance of the artistically intolerable, how unassailable, how triumphant it is ! And for supremacy in the plastic arts, no one, I suppose, would turn to England or any northern nation. They are of the South. In these arts races nourished in the Mediterranean tradition alone have succeeded supremely, races in touch with the gorgeous East, educated through the ancient trade routes before the dawn of history by Assyria and Babylon in the values of form, the values of colour, and under skies where form took its sharpest outlines and colour its purest tones. Nobody in the world thinks of the Englishman as a born artist ; does anyone think of him as a born poet ? Yet the poetry is there. Matthew Arnold, in his famous and engaging discourses at Oxford, explained its presence by dwelling on the Celtic element in the English nature. We were a mixed people, fortunately blended, and the Celt in us resolved the mystery. He it was who redeemed our race from Germanism, gave to our poetry its sense for style, and made Shakespeare and Milton possible. This admirable speculation seems to stand where it did, for the ethnologists have not yet convinced each other, and the rest of us can but continue to speculate. The pursuit of certainty is most fascinating in studies that least permit of it, but we still must echo Arnold's cry—' And we then, what are we ? what is England ? ' The hour certainly befriends the Celtic theory, for it seems likely that we shall henceforth count ourselves even less Teutonic than we used to believe, and readily, all of us, become Britons or Normans. If, however, our literary history is made in some ways more intelligible by thinking of the Celt, the rest of our history is made less intelligible by thinking of him. *They went forth to the war, but they always fell* will hardly serve as a sentence to illumine English history. And the talent for affairs, for political compromise, for colonial enterprise—these, I suppose, we must ascribe to the Normans, and it would seem, then, that, by some ingenious division of labour, to the descendants of one race Nature had entrusted the poetic, and to those of another the practical business of the nation. The hypothesis, charming though it be, awaits verification. So rapidly, too, have the researches of the linguistic scholars been succeeded by those of the anthropologists that for races of whom Arnold had never heard a share may yet be claimed in our national achievements. Meanwhile to lay an exact finger upon the contribution of any race to our national history is too hazardous a venture, and it seems preferable to proceed in a simpler fashion, to connect our poetry more directly with English character and history as we know them.

The governing characteristics of the Englishman are not greatly in dispute. His sturdy nationalism, for example, has all along and everywhere been acknowledged. The earliest proof of it lies in the 'withdrawal,' to use Bishop Creighton's word, the 'withdrawal' of England from that marvellous fraternity of the Middle Ages, feudal and Catholic Europe. By the fourteenth century she had become a separate nation, committed to the voyage of her own destiny. At a price the Englishman purchased his freedom. Deliberately he stood aloof from the centre, from the main stream of ideas, from the light and warmth of European civility. He remained, as it were, the country cousin of the family, preferring, one might say, the rough, free, out-of-doors life to the elegance and refinements with the accompanying restraints of the town. He declined the advantages of the best Latin society. Unattracted by the mediæval vision of a united Christendom, of races held together by common acceptance of the same laws, the same religious creeds and observances, the same chivalric ideals, he set over against the abstract perfections of this dazzling scheme his own liberty, his own habits, his own interests. He had no eye for the beauty of a universal, an ideal order. His talent has ever been for life rather than logic. Of general principles, because they tend to imprison the individual, he is suspicious. 'My case is always a special case. Why should I be treated as one of a number, I, who am unlike all the rest?' He preferred, too, the old 'laws of St. Edward' to any legislative novelties, his own priests and bishops to foreigners, his own language to

Norman French. He knew his mind and achieved his ends, not indeed so much by way of argument as by patient indifference to argument, and the gradual development of national consciousness only stiffened his original prejudices. His country satisfied him as the best, his race as manifestly the bravest and the handsomest in the world. To go his own way, think his own thoughts, conduct his own undertakings is all an Englishman asks, or used to ask, and if he interferes in the affairs of others, it is only that he may not be interfered with. By this early withdrawal from the comity of European nations, England led the van in liberty but brought up the rear in civility. For while they advanced in the social arts, in literary and artistic sense, while they seized upon and familiarized themselves with Renaissance ideals, she continued to pour her best energies into practical channels, fighting within her own borders to lay the foundations of civil liberty and on all the seas to secure her commercial and yet unseen imperial future.

The career of Milton illustrates the national character, its practical and positive quality. If ever an Englishman was a born artist, it was he. Yet perceiving on his Italian journey that, in his own words, ' a way was opening for the establishment of real liberty,' he is at once aroused, forgoes his studies, abandons his Muse, sacrifices all his ambitions, and gives the best years of his life to the cause of political freedom. How characteristically English that is ! This then, as Cardinal Newman said, is ' the people for private enterprise,' and a little later added with equal truth, ' a government is their natural foe.' In his private capacity the Englishman owes nothing to the state, he asks nothing from it, he hardly cares for its protection.

> Their governors they count such dangerous things
> That 'tis their custom to affront their kings.

The less government the better has been his consistent creed for the weaker the central authority the wider field for his own energy and talent. The conviction that the state was made for Englishmen and not Englishmen for the state made it at times his unwilling servant; he was careful that it should never be his master. And the empire? Nothing of course could be further from the truth than to ascribe either its origin or growth to the organized and sustained effort of any central authority. Neither planned for nor foreseen, it is, as Newman so eloquently describes, the work of individuals, men acting for the most part without other warrant than their own energetic inclinations —merchants, travellers, explorers, adventurers, colonists—whose unauthorized and personal enterprises, multitudinous, daring, resourceful, contributed without conscious design to the astonishing consummation. The state, so far from encouraging, often disowned or disclaimed responsibility for these individual performances, and when it lent them support did so with reluctant tardiness. Is it surprising that such unconsidered empire-building appears to exasperate and bewilder nations accustomed to act only through their organized authorities, nations which move in drilled and disciplined masses at the command of their rulers towards a goal foreseen and predetermined?

We have then this withdrawal from the centre and this ineradicable independence as facts in our political history. Turn to our literary history and what do we find? That here too the Englishman went his own way. One cannot of course picture him as a recluse, as so aloof and wrapped up in himself as to refuse all intercourse with his neighbours or concern with their ideas. The truth is that by this very withdrawal, this aloofness, he rendered himself very susceptible to the influence of these ideas when they reached him. And at seasons they did reach him, borne across the straits like strange perfumes, all the charm of social grace and refinement, of literature and learning and the arts. The country cousin of whom I spoke, rarely a visitor to town, finds its fashions none the less novel and attractive on that account. Yet in the main he goes his own way, a contented rustic. As Pope puts it—

> We, brave Britons, foreign laws despised
> And kept unconquer'd and unciviliz'd.

Doubtless, for example, the advocates of the ancient rules, as recommended to the Elizabethan playwrights by the elegant and accomplished Sir Philip Sidney, had the best of the argument. The English case remained for long, at least, without defenders. Yet the dramatists, Shakespeare among them, continued to write plays which were 'neither right tragedies nor right comedies, mingling kings and clowns,' observing the 'rules neither of honest civility nor of skilful poetry . . . faulty both in place and time, the two necessary companions of all corporal actions.' Thus, as might be expected, the country cousin has, as Sidney called our drama, 'an unmannerly daughter showing a bad education.' Doubtless also the quantitative metres so persuasively urged upon Spenser by his friend Gabriel Harvey had much to be said for them. 'I like your late Englishe hexameters so exceedingly well,' wrote Spenser, 'that I also enure my pen sometime in that kinde.' Yes, but he writes *The Faerie Queene* in stanzas. The poet Campion is not only convinced of the superiority of the classical metres, he is enthusiastic about them, and produces a treatise in their favour to convince others. But for himself he is careful not to follow whither the argument leads. He is an Englishman, he turns his back upon it, his practice is better than his theory, and he composes verses, none more charming, that are ruled by rime and accent. Or take the matter of an academy. 'It imputes no little disgrace to our Nation,' wrote Richard Carew in 1605, 'that others have so many Academyes, and wee none at all.' Such was also the opinion of Edmund Bolton, whose society, had it been founded in 1616, planned to include great names, Chapman and Drayton and Ben Jonson. Dryden, too, favoured the design when revived in 1664, Evelyn spoke up for it in a letter to Pepys, Bishop Sprat urged it again in 1667, and Swift in 1712. Admirable reasons were advanced for the project, which never lacked friends, yet without opposition it withered, nor does the cause of its ill-success clearly emerge until Dr. Johnson set it forth half a century later in his uncompromising fashion. What is the root of his objection? Simply that the less government we have the better, in literature as in politics. 'It was a proposal,' said he, 'which I, who can never wish to see dependence multiplied, hope the spirit of English liberty will hinder or destroy.'

As for the profits of this independence this 'spirit of English liberty,' we may claim with some confidence that it preserved, in full vigour and vitality, the originality, the genius native to the race. Whatever the dangers of contact with more facile, more fluent, more subtile, more social peoples, these were avoided. In many ways they were real enough. 'The Englishman Italianate is the devil incarnate' ran the Elizabethan proverb. 'Our countrymen usually bring three things with them out of Italy,' it was said, 'a naughty conscience, an empty purse, and a weak stomach.' If the country cousin escaped moral he escaped also intellectual dangers, too close an imitation, too slavish a pursuit of Latin graces and refinements. This, too, we may claim, and with great assurance, that in trusting to their own experiences and reflections our poets and men of letters drew upon the only authentic sources of inspiration, and that the strength of our poetry is due to this trust. The best school for poetry as for everything else is the school of personal experience. We may say with truth that the fortune of our literature was made by attendance on this school, we may praise our writers for their originality and variety, but there are other qualities for which we cannot praise them. Too frequently they lack, and our most friendly critics complain of it, restraint, lucidity, finish, shapeliness. Allow that inspiration is less frequently wanting, yet he who trusts to inspiration, one discovers, too often trusts to improvisation, and how much of our poetry is little better than improvisation. And so foreign critics speak, to our surprise, of ' the rude but splendid Muse of the Britons.' If we expect from a book that it should partake of the character of a work of art—and we should expect it—that it should resemble a picture or a statue, a chapel rather than an outhouse or barn, then we require a finished product which excludes the ill-considered, the irrelevant, the haphazard ; we require a respect for words, we ask that it should avoid verbosity and save our time. But, if we look for these qualities, how often English books disappoint us. And when posterity, most inexorable of critics, gets to work, the evidence for inspiration must indeed be overwhelming if inspiration be asked to excuse verbosity and shapelessness. Our literature has developed in conformity with our national character and we must take what it gives us. It has given us, for example, the novel, the most modern of literary forms, in which we have been specially prolific. How congenial is the novel to our temperament ! Here there are no restraints, no laws have been prescribed for its government ; it revels in freedom, exalts sentiment, rejoices in the diffuse, despises verbal economy and achieves the very perfection of the amorphous. I do not know how it may be with others, but I find myself constantly in agreement with the sentiment of Amiel : 'Keep your vats, your must, your dregs to yourselves : I want wine fully made, wine which will sparkle in the glass.'

To return to my thesis. An instinct for emancipation, for a free passage everywhere, appears clearly in our literature as in our national character, so that we are and have always been willing to pardon anything to genius, to trust to its happy moments, to overlook its vagaries, to permit every man to be a law unto himself. The apparition of Shakespeare, who never blotted a line, blinds us to the virtues of restraint, of exactness, of order, virtues which, but for our insularity and withdrawal from close contact with Latin culture, might at a price have been ours. Our history shows that above all things we prize originality and independence of mind, that we prize even the eccentric as evidence of spontaneity and truth to nature. We delight in these qualities and are correspondingly indifferent to the disciplined and deliberate side of art. Nothing so charmed the spectators of Elizabethan tragedy as the exalted, the towering in character, the superman like Marlowe's Tamburlaine, storming across the stage to the capture of Babylon in a chariot drawn by conquered kings, Caesar, who bestrode ' this narrow world like a Colossus,' or Antony in whose livery ' walk'd crowns and crownets.' Nothing so charmed the spectators of comedy as the extravagant, the unconventional in character or person, the vast bulk and uncontrollable exuberance of Falstaff, the whimsicalities of Touchstone. It is their humours we prize in men, not the qualities which unite but the idiosyncrasies which distinguish them from each other. We prefer a parti-coloured world. Nor is ugliness excluded. That is tolerable, even welcome, provided it be expressive of individuality. So much so, indeed, that with us an author may flourish on his very infirmities. Why eliminate what unfailingly attracts an audience ? This preference has persisted with us, and will probably continue to persist. Not only are we content to be pleased we ' know not why and care not wherefore,' not only do many of our most talented authors, like Browning, for example, in his *Ring and the Book*, or Mr. Hardy in his *Dynasts*, works of genius if you will, make these shapeless, verbose things, but we are satisfied with them and praise them. We must all gladly suffer in the cause of freedom, nothing is so well worth suffering for, but may we not, now and again perhaps, confess to our sufferings, may we not, claiming an English privilege, complain that we pay a high price for it ?

' The world that I regard,' said Sir Thomas Browne, ' is myself.' There again we have the characteristic note. He owns no other authority. ' What do I think and feel,' he asks, ' what shall I do ? ' not ' What are the thoughts, feelings, susceptibilities, what are the counsels of other men ? ' Goethe in his conversations with Eckermann praised the English for their courage in being themselves, in following out the bent of their natures. He praised, too, ' their ease and confidence among foreigners, as if they were lords everywhere and the whole world belonged to them.' Times have changed, and Goethe's countrymen no longer praise these qualities. They have ceased to be English virtues and have become English vices. Still, whatever they are, whether virtues or vices, they remain national characteristics. When he writes, our foreign critics assure us, the Englishman gives the impression that he is wholly preoccupied with his own thoughts and feelings, and expresses them first and last for his own satisfaction. ' In London,' said an eighteenth-century Frenchman, ' everyone assumes just what character he pleases ; there you surprise no one by being yourself.' When he turns author he does not change. Men of other and more sociable nations may write to delight or persuade their readers, the Englishman writes that he may converse with himself. He wishes to contemplate his own image in the mirror, to paint, as it were, his own portrait. Clearly in this undertaking a man has less need to imitate others, to consider the example of others, the less need, that is, to follow the rules, the tradition. For what is the tradition ? What is it but the body of doctrine, accepted by previous writers, taking stock of earlier successes and failures ? Tradition in any art is nothing more than the capitalized experience of its students. If, then, we write to please or persuade others the value of the tradition is evident : it professes to show just how this success may be achieved. If on the other hand we write to please ourselves it is much less evident, for who can guide us to this result better than our own inclinations ?

Respect for the tradition, for the opinion of others made French civilization the wonder and admiration of the world. In French literature deference to authority, regard for the universal, sympathy with the wishes and susceptibilities of men at large, a care for social requirements meet us at every turn. It charms by putting every one of us at his ease, by asking our good opinion, by taking trouble to meet us half-way, by introducing us to the pleasant society of like-minded neighbours. If ever writers could say that they ' only give back to the public what they had borrowed from it,' remarks M. Brunetière, French writers may say so. English writers on the other hand borrow nothing from the public, everything from themselves.

I do not for the moment attempt to sum up the gains and losses. This much appears certain. With less respect for the tradition, less for the rules, with a far less sensitive artistic conscience, the Englishman was somehow more successful in poetry. He yields to his brilliant neighbours in some but not in all, not even, it would appear, in the most essential points. Where art is faulty there may be insight, and vision, a greater thing, may outrange social sense. Still, so valuable is tradition, the body of educated opinion, that without it even genius is almost powerless. To protect oneself against false prophets, against intellectual charlatans, even against clap-trap and fustian is not an easy matter. The intellectual atmosphere is always thick with confused ideas, blurred images, incoherent emotions. Against a man who stands alone false standards will almost certainly prevail. When we stand together, one generation with another, we are in less danger of mistaking for excellence what is far from excellence, of becoming the dupes of temporary fashion. Our national horror of pedantry, of ink-horn terms is justifiable, but respect for the tradition is not pedantry. Without it and the institutions which preserve it how precarious would be our intellectual balance. Our universities and learned societies have no more important function than to protect the nation from a belief in the second-rate, the inferior men and inferior products.

Poetry, least of all arts and sciences, one is accustomed to think, demands knowledge and technical equipment. Poets, we imagine, are happy and irresponsible beings, directed by divine instinct, fortunately free from the dire necessity of

preparation or labour imposed upon other men. Wholly
guided by inspiration, little, we suppose, can be done for them,
they are born not made. Yet call to mind the eminent names.
Observe how seldom even in this region, sacred to genius, the
impulses of inspiration suffice. Few indeed have been the
English poets who reached without a guide the summits of
fame, few who were not studious disciples of their predecessors,
few even, explain it as you please, who were unsupported by
a prosaic university education or its equivalents. It would be
as vain to seek, we are nevertheless agreed, for the secret of our
success in poetry in a regard for the rules of art, the body of
received opinion, as in a native or deep-seated sense of beauty.
And in truth if poetry were primarily a matter of art, or again
if it were the offspring of wit and the social sense, English
success in it would be inexplicable. But, say what some critics
will, it is not primarily a matter of art at all. One cannot
enter the temple, as Plato said, by the help of art. No, we
may answer, nor yet without it. Briefly, let us say, success in
poetry is attained when finished and arresting expression is
given to some moving thought or experience. We must look
for it, therefore, where thought and word, inspiration and art
are found together, at a confluence of streams. It will be
found, I believe, chiefly in our history when in the traffic of
thought, the intellect of one race meets the intellect of another,
at the moments of their most fruitful union.

There have been many definitions of poetry. From among
them let me take Newman's. Poetry, said Newman, is ' originality energizing in the world of beauty.' By common consent
the English have been distinguished by their originality and
energy. History shows, indeed, how much of their energy
was devoted to the preservation or protection of this originality,
how jealously the right to exercise it was guarded. Originality
and energy are there, native to them, splendid and conspicuous
talents. But the talent for beauty, the sense for beauty, like
that of the Greeks pervading the whole of life, the extreme

sensitiveness to every breath of loveliness whether in nature or language or art, that talent and that sensitiveness we can claim neither for our ancestors nor for ourselves. The sense for beauty is not native to us and needs kindling. For this, if for no other reason, the study of Greek literature and art, where we are at the fountain head of beauty, should be of all literatures and arts the most precious to our countrymen. But, if a sense of beauty be not native to us, an essential element as required in Newman's definition is lacking. The sense needs, as I have said, kindling, and if for the flame that kindled it we go in search among the constituent races that produced ' that heterogeneous thing an Englishman,' we plunge into the unknown, we elaborate a speculative psychology. If one says ' England is England and France is France ' one is clearly enough understood, but in attempting to penetrate far behind these terms nothing is easier than to lose one's footing. Attempting to pass behind the term ' England,' Matthew Arnold could see no brilliant prospect for our poetry in the characteristics of the Anglo-Saxon, and quotes the old Irish poem which derides him—' For dullness the creeping Saxons.' He turned, therefore, as we have seen, to the Celt and put his trust in Celtic romance and love of beauty. Possibly he was right, but without committing ourselves to a perilous decision here, let us take a stand on firmer ground, on the notion of the crossing of ideas rather than of races, the fertilization, if we may call it so, of one type of genius by another type.

By withdrawal from the closer intimacy offered her with Latin civilization England preserved nationality, point of view, the distinctive flavour of her own qualities. She preserved originality, and the flood of native energy, derived from many tributary races, flowed into a thousand practical channels. While to her southern neighbours England seemed the fitting home of a restless, melancholy people, inhabiting a country of pale sunshine, blurred landscapes and unwilling soil, a clumsy people, unlettered, mannerless, made ' terrible and bold,' as

Defoe said, by their climate, but otherwise negligible, she was far from intellectually idle. So late as the seventeenth century Louis XIV asked whether there existed any writers or scholars in England. Yet in truth for centuries, unassisted, untutored by ancient sages, guided mainly by their own instincts, the English had for themselves faced the old human problems. Thrown upon their native resources, they had been and were not ill-content to be their own prophets and teachers, their own philosophers. Though so late in history, with ancient civilizations behind them, never very closely in touch with these civilizations, they encountered the world with virgin minds. Nor is it wonderful that, so occupied, they placed life before art. Our pre-Norman literature, like *Beowulf*, harsh and untutored though it be, is firmly rooted in experience. How clearly it sees life for what it is and how fearlessly meets it ! It faces the world with a philosophy unborrowed from books and yet perfectly suited to that world. Compare *Beowulf* with Homer, and you may safely claim Homer's superiority in beauty and poetic quality, not so safely his superiority in masculine vigour and truth. ' Better it is that a man should avenge his friend than that he should greatly mourn. Every one of us comes to his end, let him who will achieve renown, leaving a famous name.'—' Not a foot's length shall I give back before the warden of the barrow, but it shall be for us at the rampart as fate, the disposer of all men, may decree.' Who is speaking here ? One might fancy Homer himself. Or at a later date compare Dante and Langland, visionaries both, not far separated from each other in time. Where does the Englishman yield to the Italian ? Yield to him he must at every point of art, grace, finish, sweetness, dignity. Yet assuredly, half barbaric as he seems, a wild and rugged figure beside the learned and aristocratic Dante, Langland is not less impressive in his fiery intensity, in his unyielding grasp of realities. Of his own world he is as complete a master, nor does a feature of it escape him. He knows his England and

probes it to the quick, but the world of beauty he never enters.
That is where Langland fails as a poet. Where there is no
beauty there is no poetry. That is where his countryman and
contemporary Chaucer so magnificently succeeds. Chaucer
succeeds because his eyes have been opened to another vision.
Over against the imperfections of the world of humanity he
perceived the perfections of the world of art. He had been,
we may say, at school in France and at the university in Italy.
Yet if poetry is not fundamentally a matter of art but a matter
of mental and emotional experiences, and of the variety and
intensity of these experiences, this preoccupation with life may
prove the best preparation for it. Then any man who has
adventured far on this voyage, who loves, in Chapman's phrase,
' to have his sails filled with a lusty wind,' who has been moved
and thrilled by the great spectacle is potentially a poet. And
what strikes one in comparing our own with the poetry of
any other modern nation, the last five centuries of our literature
with that of Spain, of France or of Italy, is the wealth and
variety of its themes. Their themes are on the whole slighter
and fewer, their poetry has its roots in love and war, in romantic
subjects generally, and is far less occupied with the whole range
of human experience than ours. English writers have forced,
we might say, more of the prose of life to become poetry.
They have gathered the ' pleasant honey of the Muses ' where
flowers seemed least abundant. They have usually escaped too,
so intent are they upon the main issues of thought, that last
poetic infirmity, the elaborate chasing of the cup that contains
nothing. Rarely have they offered us wine without body.
What thoughts have not passed through the minds of these
men, what feelings have they not experienced ? How vast the
field touched with emotion is there, how many characters
studied, humours explored, speculations pursued, passions
expressed ! How varied, in a word, the mental energy and
activity they display. Shakespeare, its greatest author, is typical
of our literature at large. Not without faults of taste, never

sure-footed even in his finest passages, he yet easily eclipses all others in the breadth of his human interests. Shakespeare is what he is, one need have no reservations in saying it, not as an artist but as a citizen of the world. True to his race he never shows himself anxious about the rules, but rejoicing in freedom reviews the length and breadth of existence and stretches out his rod from pole to pole of human nature. There is nothing accidental in this, he pursues the curve determined by his English bias.

Everywhere then our writers are observers and thinkers first and poets afterwards. When they fail it is because they are without wings, never because they are without ideas. Take Chaucer, who was, as I have said, at school in France and at the university in Italy. In him the English genius flowered when the observant, reflective spirit, which had explored human experience, met the genius of the South and had revealed to it the persuasive charm of form and symmetry, of rhythm and order and the craft of words. So with the ' new company of courtly-makers ' in the sixteenth century : ' they travelled into Italy,' says Puttenham, ' and there tasted the sweet and stately measures and style of the Italian poesy.' In our history success in poetry is met with where a current of ideas not distinctively English flows into the main stream of national thought and disturbs it. From the ripples and eddies that are then formed, from the agitation and disquiet, we judge the presence of a new force. In the ferment created by the clashing of opposites, under the stimulus of unfamiliar emotions, the originality and energy of the English spirit blossoms, the sturdy tree of independent thought puts forth flower and fruit. At every point where our poetry rises to great elevations the native strain is crossed by another. Tempering its gravity with extreme sweet the high austere soul of Spenser looks out from a palace of splendours, the voluptuous splendours of intoxicating Italy. In Marlowe England meets full face the gale of Renaissance passions. The shining perfection of Greek art passed like an arrow through the harness of Milton's Puritanism. To Dryden and Pope the exquisite shapeliness, the logic and precision required by the French spirit flung an unceasing challenge. From ' the horns of Elfland ' strange airs floated to the ears of Gray and his successors.

But, some one will say, how comes it that the distinction of English literature is not in prose rather than poetry ? The mind of a practical and energetic people accustomed to take what is offered, to deal directly with the matter in hand, will express itself more naturally and completely in a plain and simple fashion, the fashion of prose, rather than in a heightened and elaborate fashion, the fashion of poetry. It will be more at its ease in the field of reason than of imagination. Yet we know the opposite to be the truth. Practical and lovers of freedom as they are, revolting against all checks and limitations, English writers have been somehow assisted by the very checks and limitations which poetry imposes. Its strictness helps rather than hinders them. Wordsworth, to take a striking example, was helped not hindered by the boundaries of the sonnet. The more the stream of his thought was confined within banks, the less it was permitted to overflow into un-restricted areas, the more powerful became the current. And what is true of Wordsworth is true of English writers in general. Is Shakespeare less effective in his sonnets, or less effective in the plays where he permits himself least freedom, than else-where in his works ? No one will say so. But that is not all. English thought in a surprising and surpassing measure associates itself with emotion. I shall not here ask the interest-ing question, how far it is possible to think without feeling at the same time, how far what one may describe as pure thinking can be conducted at all, thinking, that is, largely or altogether disentangled or dissociated from feeling. Setting aside this fascinating question we may assert that with us more of emotion enters into our thinking than with most other peoples, we throw the whole of our natures, as it were, into the process, which is, with us, not an excited or rapid, but a robust one. We do not think so lucidly and logically as the French. Everyone must acknowledge the French superiority in that respect. Yet because our thought is more highly charged with feeling it is the richer in consequence. It is obscurer but more glowing, less exact because more luxuriant. And our poetry profits by it. Indeed since poetry for most of its lovers provides confused delight rather than a pure intellectual pleasure, we are the better fitted to excel in it. Poetry, said Coleridge, with great acuteness, ' gives more pleasure when only generally and not perfectly understood.' The mood of poetry is never the logical or analytic mood, never the mood in which we approach the investigation of truth, but always that in which we enjoy some accepted truth. And even our prose writers, so continuously is their thought accompanied and supported by feeling, are rarely capable of presenting a subject in the dry cool light of the isolated intelligence. Our best prose, as the critics frequently inform us, is imaginative, inspired by sympathy with its subject, by warmth of heart rather than by the spirit of scientific enquiry.

Thus then the connexion between our national character and the achievements of our poets may partly be traced. And what may we conclude ? We may conclude in the first place that to nothing as a people do we owe so much as to the spirit of liberty, the soul, as it were, of our national life. Everywhere and at all times it has inspired and directed our activities. We do not exist as a nation in order to excel in any one respect, to make ourselves powerful, or artistic or anything else. We prefer to leave a wide field for the development of all forms and types of excellence ; not by the subordination of the rest to compass any one end, but rather to keep open the avenues to many. As a people we are for excluding no quality for the sake of another, exalting no single virtue as super-excellent or final. It is not in our nature to enslave ourselves for scientific method or artistic success or military strength. We wish, and

we are constantly blamed for it, to be men rather than pro-
fessionals or specialists, whether artists, savants, or soldiers. We
place the possession of freedom before all other aims. In its
defence we have made many sacrifices in the past and are
prepared to make further sacrifices. So precious a thing must
be preserved at all costs. But we must also conclude that
whether in life or literature freedom has its dangers. In the
field of foreign politics, for example, as our present situation
proves, a free people is at manifest, in war it may easily be at
a fatal, disadvantage. Though possessed of ample resources it
may be suddenly struck down by an envious rival organized
not so much for peace as for war, by some nation which is
nothing else than an army ever prepared to strike, a nation
under a strong central government, ruling as if from the heavens,
to which it is perfectly submissive. ' If we prefer to meet
danger with a light heart but without training,' said Pericles
in addressing the Athenians, ' with a courage which is gained
by habit and not enforced by law, are we not greatly the
gainers ? ' We have hitherto held the same view. The
reflection has, however, been forced upon us that England is
no longer as remote from Europe as in former times and can
no longer withdraw itself from European concerns. As freedom of speech, of criticism, the free exchange of ideas, can
alone help us to the best thought, the best ideas, so, if we aspire
to lead the world, no other course than to preserve our free
political institutions seems open. Yet to play so splendid a
rôle is to occupy a dangerous post. Nor will our insular
position serve us in the future to pursue our national aims
undisturbed as it has served us in the past. In art and literature,
too, freedom has its perils. No one who knows our literature
will deny this, will deny that it has suffered from disorder and
caprice, from obscurity and eccentricity, in a word from too
much liberty rather than from too much rigour and formality.
If freedom, however, means anything it means tolerance, and
if tolerance is to be real we must, for the sake of the blessing

of liberty, put up with every kind of disagreeable absurdity, with works manifestly in the worst taste, and ridiculous demands upon us to admire them, with the personal vagaries of well-intentioned but ill-educated persons who force themselves upon our attention, and too often succeed in capturing the public, in degrading its judgment and confusing its conscience. In praising freedom one should remember that it does not sanctify all that it permits. In politics freedom such as ours may lead to ruin unless as a people we retain our sagacity, good sense enough not to be imposed upon, not to be hoodwinked ; in art, unless we make habitual reference to the tradition, the capitalized experience of the past, it leads to our being in Renan's phrase ' devoured by charlatanism.'

What form our political institutions should take in the future if we are to preserve our freedom, how we may best protect it, though an attractive theme, is here beyond us. But in the world of letters, limiting ourselves to that, when we cast our eyes abroad and behold the new and greater England beyond two oceans, we should, I think, dwell more upon the qualities in which we are deficient, which we have found difficult of attainment, less upon those natural to us. And that for two reasons. The qualities natural to us need not be insisted upon, they will make their appearance without any conscious effort. Independence of mind, trust in happy inspirations, dislike of formality and pedantry, these characteristics we are not likely to lose. It was for a very brief period in our history that we seemed in danger of preferring Waller to Shakespeare. That is the first, and not a negligible reason, but the second out-weighs it. The qualities that come less easily to us have acquired a new value. If, and it seems probable for some time to come, the language of these islands be accepted as the standard, if our writers at home be looked to for guidance by the writers of English abroad, then, whether in prose or poetry, the merits of a scrupulous style demand reconsideration. A style of the centre, less highly charged with personal qualities,

marked by its respect for words, its exactness and lucidity, its
finish and purity should, to meet the circumstances, rise in our
estimation. If our writers aspire to be in any measure the
schoolmasters of the English world they must become lovers
of restraint and proportion, of shapeliness and verbal economy.
The secret way to the reader's heart does not lie through self-
indulgence, indifference to form and finish, disdain of discipline
and the labour of the file. Nor does the way to permanence
lie through them. Emancipation is not everything. Negligence and indolence are too often its accompaniments. Dryden,
not the least careful of our authors, was, says Dr. Johnson, ' no
rigid judge of his own pages ; he seldom struggled after supreme
excellence, but snatched in haste what was within his reach.'
With such a temper, and it is the English temper, more especially since the torrent of print daily increases in the world, and
must still further increase, since we are all writers now, with
such a temper we shall have a hard task to protect our language
from deterioration and decay. The praise given to Dryden,
that he found English poetry brick and left it marble, praise
too great even for Dryden, can never again be adjudged to
any English poet. The smooth and bright perfection of marble,
the substance in which the qualities of the Greek spirit found
their exquisite symbol, is beyond the reach of our language
and our poetry. The most we can hope for them, and that
only if we submit to uncongenial discipline, is the strength and
durability of bronze.

Chatterton

Chatterton's is not one of the far-sounding names, and you may be surprised at my choice of subject. But we are met to honour Warton, and to think of Warton is to be reminded of Chatterton, for whom the first historian of our poetry had so strong a sympathy and so deep an admiration. A strange and lonely lad, his position in our literature is not less strange and lonely. He died before he had reached his eighteenth birthday, and yet climbed to a niche in the temple of fame ; the youngest poet, I fancy, who in any era or country has a place among the immortals. Poets are usually remembered for their poetry. Chatterton certainly was a poet of the authentic breed, yet he left little or nothing of high intrinsic importance, no familiar stanzas, no memorable lines. His was a promise rather than a performance. But he has a place in literary history. He marks the turn of the year. ' At any rate,' wrote Browning :

> ' At any rate I have loved the season
> Of art's spring birth, so dim and dewy,
> My sculptor is Nicolo the Pisan,
> My painter who but Cimabue.'

There is something of the same morning fragrance in Chatterton. It has, too, been claimed for him that he was the true discoverer of the metrical principle employed in *Christabel*, that he was the father of the Romantic school, that he showed the way to Scott and Coleridge, Byron and Keats. These are interesting claims. They have, however, elsewhere been discussed and justice has been done to them. It is for another reason that I venture to recall this slight boyish figure to your memories. His times were not poetic times. Were they any the worse for that ? When we think of Chatterton it seems natural to inquire once more what precisely is the nature and value of poetry. Or

48

again, have we in our own age of enlightenment any pressing need for this peculiar form of human activity? I occasionally ask myself whether, if we woke some morning to find the whole body of English poetry had vanished, whether the nation would be horror-stricken, plunged in irremediable grief? Some professors and critics would no doubt be placed in a situation of extreme inconvenience. But would the country be inconsolable, our neighbours all in tears? Might we not get along pretty comfortably with reason, and science and common sense, and without poetry?

Chatterton was born, you remember, into the famous 'age of prose and reason,' 'our understanding age,' as Addison complacently called it, very conscious of its good sense, and the inestimable blessings of good sense. The men of that time, it was universally felt, were to be congratulated. They never ceased, indeed, congratulating themselves. And not without cause. Who could dispute the happiness of their lot? Had not Europe left behind the stupidities of the Dark Ages, escaped from the misery and degradation in which she had for centuries been steeped? Reason bid fair to prevail at length over ignorance and superstition. The Royal Society, that magnificent monument of British genius, founded in 1662, pointed the way to vast extensions of knowledge, and science had already begun to work her wonders. The new Golden Age, the age of the calm, clear, invincible intelligence seemed at hand. Equal to all undertakings, it might well be expected not only to unravel the mysteries of nature, but even to transform human society. It was a gallant creed and a cheering prospect. The future held all the promises. Chatterton arrests attention in that, as a child, instinctively and without instruction, guided by some inward prompting, he turns away from this promising future to the past, the repudiated past. He turns back to history. He fingers lovingly the very fringes of its outworn and tattered garments, the old black letter and the yellow parchment. Inspired by what his own age held in contempt, he found in the dim splendours, the colours, and columns and traceries of the Gothic aisle a strong enchantment. What fetters his gaze in that quarter of the heavens ? He finds there poetry and a spiritual home. This child, in brief, made a twofold discovery. He discovered the magic of far horizons, and a secret in the Middle Ages overlooked by his sophisticated and enlightened contemporaries. So intense, as we shall see, were his mediæval sympathies, so inborn, intuitive, untaught, that one might fancy him astray in time, born out of season ; or as a soul returning to the world, bringing with him, as Plato feigned, memories and attachments from a former existence. But how, then, account for similar sympathies in others of his own day, in Warton, and Gray and Walpole ? They, too, felt a need for something more than the age of reason supplied. What is singular in Chatterton is that, where the rest, even Warton himself, had their hesitations, their moments of doubt and apology, his was an untutored and overwhelming passion, an obsession.

These correspondences in mood between far-separated ages have a curious interest. The mind appears at intervals to make a kind of return upon itself. Ponder its successive phases, and you perceive that, like everything else in nature, it has its rhythms. You observe a pulse in things human, a recurring beat in the heart of the world. Old thoughts recur in new generations. The rate of the mind's pulsations is not, however, easily reckoned, nor have the wave-lengths of history, though suspected, been so far mathematically determined. Still it is, I suppose, within every one's experience that here and there in some distant age he finds a natural friend, a mind in tune with his own. Plutarch takes our fancy, or Carpaccio charms us above his fellows. As with individuals, so with times. Bridges of understanding and sympathy there are which connect periods separated, perhaps, by as much as or more than a millennium. The men of the Renaissance turned back the leaves of the record fifteen hundred years to take delight in Pagan antiquity. And how close the analogy between our own times and those of Lucian 'too striking,' as Leslie Stephen said, ' to be overlooked.' ' A twentieth-century Englishman, a second-century Greek or Roman,' it has been remarked, ' would be much more at home in each other's century, if they had the gift of tongues, than in most of those which have intervened.' The interest of the mediæval revival, its return to the past, is the greater in that to the eighteenth-century intellectuals it appeared fantastic, a fall from grace, almost indecent, and certainly ridiculous. Here were men in an enlightened age prepared to jettison all their gains, to parley with the irrational and admire the preposterous. It might have been amusing had it not been alarming, for it savoured of lunacy.

' Men who think, and what is more, men who have taste,' wrote Voltaire, ' count but four centuries in the history of the world.' It is no very flattering estimate of human existence. And what centuries were worthy, and alone worthy, of the thoughtful man's consideration ? Simply the centuries which had produced the art and literature of Greece and Rome. In the life of the human race there had been a single lucid interval, the bright classic day after primitive barbarism and before the ' long Gothic night ' set in. In that brief hour the mind had been at work. There, and there only, might be found the fruits of intelligence, all that made life worth living—law, philosophy, art, letters, social refinement—in a word, civilization.

For the rest of the story, it was negligible. In the remaining centuries men, no doubt in millions, had passed across the stage, but how destitute of any value to succeeding generations their pitiful proceedings. Why then re-enter the jungle of unreason from which mankind had so painfully emerged ? Why concern oneself with the senseless practices of uncouth and unlettered barbarians ? To what purpose an enquiry into the doings of savages ? In 1752, the year of Chatterton's birth, educated Europe was substantially of Voltaire's opinion. Athens it knew and Rome it knew. Around and beyond the classic pale, that noble, cultivated garden of the intellect, stretched beyond sight the forbidding wilderness, a welter of confusion. The Middle Ages bore, as was natural, the full brunt of this aristocratic disdain. The barbarism of primitive tribes might be overlooked and pitied. But the Goths and Vandals, as the destroyers of civilization, were from the humanist standpoint the villains of the piece, and as every one knows, the term Gothic became in its vocabulary a term of contempt.

How great are the triumphs of reason, and how great, too, are its failures ! From history it shrinks back in alarm. Nor can we refuse our pity to its disciples on their passage through this world of ours, a world so manifestly mad. The orderly movements of nature, the regular procession of the heavens, the measurable behaviour of atoms and molecules afford them some satisfaction. But the thoughts, feelings, and actions of men are fantastic and wholly incalculable. History is the despair of the rationalist. From the point of view of sober reason, indeed, the humanist case is unanswerable. For it is, you may say, the case of reason itself. The eighteenth century assumed that the mediæval scene—one of the most moving scenes in the human drama, strange, pathetic, amazing, beautiful —had no significance, no value. What an assumption, indeed, and what an error ! Yes, but that age was not in search of moving scenes or human drama, of beauty, or pathos, or poetry. It was bent on understanding the world. And the Middle Ages were wholly incomprehensible. It could find no sense in them. The hopes of the eighteenth century were in the intellect. Never was there such immense confidence in reason as the master-key to open all locks. Yet something had escaped the meshes of its intellectual net which in a degree at least the Christian centuries had possessed. Pitiful as had been their estate, and for the majority, doubtless it was pitiful enough, men had then a measure of hope in their hearts and a measure of poetry in their lives. They were ignorant but they were not wholly forsaken. They were not without their deep affections, they

were not without a sense of beauty. They had a sense of the
mystery and the consolation of their dreams. But ages of
enlightenment do not deal in mysteries and dreams. The
business of reason is to dispel mysteries and put an end to dreams.
Truth and knowledge are sufficient for them, or without much
anxious enquiry they suppose them sufficient. In Chatterton's
day the star of intellect was in the ascendant, and in the galaxy
of reason, wit, satire, intelligence, shining in full splendour.
The star of poetry was below the horizon. ' D'ye see,' wrote
Walpole to a friend in 1742, ' 'tis an age most unpoetical !
'Tis even a test of wit to despise poetry.' But we are so constituted—and to quarrel with our constitution is of all things
the most useless—we, creatures of our affections, are so constituted, that even at its best and noblest reason will not suffice.
In some wide and generous interpretation of the word, poetry
is as necessary for the world's happiness as reason or knowledge,
perhaps more necessary.

Whatever view we take of the mediæval revival it clearly
illustrates a singular feature of poetry, a feature worthy attention,
its passion for the past. One might well suppose that if not
the eternally disappointing present, the open future would
afford a more alluring field for poetic minds. Upon its virgin
soil they might to their heart's content, with imagination's aid,
erect their airy palaces, or build unhindered the Utopias of their
fancies. On the contrary we know that for them, as indeed
for all of us, the past, though it be the past, and in a sense therefore matters nothing at all, yet possesses a remarkable monopoly
the monopoly of romance. What is it that captivates us in
distance, in the record of things over and done with ? We
talk of the lessons of history. Who reads history for its lessons ?
Our interest strikes far deeper. We are involved, though we
know it not, in the problem of time itself, which in our generation has risen into such peculiar prominence both in science and
philosophy. And our relations to time, if we ponder them, are
in respect of the claims of past and future upon our consideration,

very delicately balanced. The future, what is still to come, manifestly exceeds for the race in interest and importance what can never again in any living fashion, be experienced or enjoyed. It harbours, nevertheless, a defect. It is wholly void of values for the poet, the artist and historian. It contains neither æsthetic nor dramatic interest, no moving episodes, no ideals or conflicts, no plot. In its own way the future undeniably occupies a supreme, a privileged position. The thought of it is ever in our minds, governs our actions, affords room for endless and anxious speculation. It alone has power to kindle our hopes or excite our apprehensions. But it is an empty canvas. And the departed scene, once so agitated, now so still, the past, though it be wholly disarmed, from which we have nothing to expect, which can do no more, nor affect us any more, weaves none the less a spell of its own, and exerts a mysterious fascination. The crowded act, if we care to look into the magic glass of history is still with us, with authority over our thoughts, a hold upon our deepest affections.

This interest, whether rational or not, is of course neither more nor less than the supreme, the human interest which inspires alike the historian and the poet. ' Men taste well,' said Bacon, ' knowledges that are drenched in flesh and blood.' It need not surprise us, therefore, that the new birth of poetry in the mediæval revival coincides with, and is accompanied by, the awakening of the historic sense. ' There were historians in previous ages,' wrote Morley, ' but in the eighteenth century there was a special and extraordinary development in this direction.' To Chatterton and Warton, and Gray, poets all, as much as to any men, we owe this interested view over the centuries Voltaire disdained to study, this view which disclosed the values of mediæval art, architecture, and literature. And not these only. For that first look into ' the dark backward and abysm of time,' aroused the historic ardour which has since explored for us a still remoter past, cities half as old as the world, races and cultures and civilizations almost without end, whose tale is not yet complete. We begin to perceive the vast process which forms the background of our lives, the majestic pageant, the flux and reflux of the great human sea. As never before, history arrests man's astonished attention. Call it epic or drama, comedy or tragedy as you will, it recites all human experiences and vibrates with all human hopes. This then is the importance of Chatterton's vision, his passion for the past. The curtain which Voltaire had rung down begins to rise; the human drama in all its immensity to unfold itself.

Let it be confessed that from this backward look the man of reason and the man of science have derived little comfort. Human history declines to accommodate itself to their requirements and extorts from them no admiration. They have much to tell us of the magnificent theatre in which the drama is played, the superb background, the admirable stellar scenery. They dwell upon its sublime dimensions, and we are overawed by them. We are led to fancy the theatre more impressive than the play. Yet all these are mere accessories to the action and the plot, these are but the furnishings and machinery of the stage. And from the drama itself, where the eternal interest lies, the men of reason are unable to extract any intellectual satisfaction. Before history, before the astonishing procession through the ages, before its force and momentum, heights and depths of passion, tumults and catastrophes, crusades and conflicts, dreams, ideals and ambitions, before the spectacle of humanity on its march:

> ' Still nursing the unconquerable hope,
> Still clutching the inviolable shade,'

before this spectacle the intellect falls silent, and reason veils her eyes. The philosophers view it with something approaching despair. The thought of history furrowed with anxiety the calm brow of Kant, upon its irrational granite Hegel's all-subduing logic fretted itself in vain. What purpose, what meaning, lay behind this tumult of energy, this whirlpool of contending tribes and nations? For its interpretation a more powerful method than that of reason is needed, and has yet to be discovered. There is, fortunately, another manner of viewing history, not less true and more encouraging—the poet's manner. Assure the rationalist that, however far he pursues his enquiries, their goal is unattainable, convince him that the secrets of the universe are beyond hope of solution, and he will be of all men the most miserable. Not so the poet. His withers remain unwrung. He may even, lost to all sense of reason, pray God that it is so, and will remain so. He may possibly tell you that a problem solved is a problem without further interest, that a world explained is a lost and ruined world. For him, unlike the philosopher, the irrational has no terrors. So far from embarrassing his thought, the inexplicable and unfathomable exalts it. He prefers the untamed and the untameable. From the dawn of time he has consorted with the incredible and the miraculous. He contemplates without distress ' the throne of Chaos ' and ' the seat of sable-vested Night, eldest of things.' With Gorgons and Hydras he is on easy visiting terms. Gryphons, Centaurs and Chimæras eat out of his hand. In the apparent purposelessness, the terrible, the strange, the pathetic of human history, others may find painful problems for solution. The poet is well content with wonder and admiration. He says of life with Nietzsche, ' I desire thee ; it is worth while to know thee.'

I have said that Warton's sympathies with things mediæval were aroused, as Gray's were aroused, by their poetic values. Both had learning. They lived and moved, the one at Oxford, the other at Cambridge, among ancient colleges, the visible monuments of a bygone time. They were men of cultivated taste, connoisseurs, accustomed to sample literary and artistic flavours as they sampled vintages. They had but to look round them with speculative eyes. We cannot wonder that the romances took their fancy, or that Gothic architecture, its soaring and majestic structures, awoke their interest in such creations, unique in style, mysteriously wrought, and that they should ask themselves what thoughts were here enshrined, or what manner of men were their builders. Chatterton's passion was by contrast a species of miracle. It had no roots in knowledge or travel. It descended upon him in early infancy like a fire from heaven. It drove him to unremitting and solitary labours. So far from sharing his visions, probably not a boy in England could have so much as found any meaning in his religious fervour for antiquity. And a religious fervour it may justly be called.

In early childhood Chatterton exhibited none of a child's natural interests. He was dull and abstracted. It was feared that he would prove a dunce. At six years of age, however, an old French manuscript with illuminated capitals, and a black-letter Bible attracted his attention, and like a spark on powder, ignited a hidden magazine of energy. From these, refusing all other and easier print, he learned the alphabet, and so passed to general and indefatigable reading, his chosen study some niche or gallery in the great Church of St. Mary Redcliffe in Bristol, which towered above his home. With this superb building, his favourite haunt, Chatterton's childhood, indeed his whole career is inseparably associated—' the finest and most famous Parish Church in England,' said Queen Elizabeth.

For over a century, ' time out of mind ' we are told, the office of sexton had been held by members of his family, and that ' wonder of mansions,' to use his own phrase, became the fixed pivot of his thoughts, the centre of his waking dreams. I am not aware that a parallel can anywhere be found for such an influence as this. St. Mary Redcliffe dominated Chatterton's imagination. He would lie in Redcliffe meadows, gazing upon it as if entranced. It became for him the mediæval scene on which his heart was set, a crowded stage, a living chapter of history. He saw it as it stands, a glorious thing indeed, but still more wonderful as time's witness. He saw it through the centuries thronged with worshippers on high days and festivals.

Thus inextricably interwoven with its aisles and arches and monuments arose the drama to which his fancy gave such vivid life. At eight years of age Chatterton became a charity-school boy, and at fifteen he was apprenticed to a Bristol attorney. But these were no more than the external circumstances of a young life, 'Voyaging through strange seas of thought alone.' He laid hands upon all the books in Bristol libraries, 'studied best,' said his sister, 'towards the full of the moon, and would often sit up all night and write by moonlight.' Like another charity-school boy, Coleridge, he discovered for himself the high places of the mind. 'One day he might be found busily employed in the study of heraldry and English antiquities ; the next discovered him deeply engaged, confounded and perplexed amid the subtleties of metaphysical disquisition, or lost and bewildered in the abstruse labyrinths of mathematical researches ; and these in an instant again neglected and thrown aside to make room for music and astronomy, in both of which sciences his knowledge was entirely confined to theory. Even physic was not without a charm to allure his imagination, and he would talk of Galen, Hippocrates and Paracelsus with all the familiarity of a modern empiric.'

Of English poets one fancies Marlowe as his nearest kinsman in disposition and temper. There is no extant portrait of Chatterton, as there is none of Marlowe, and no comparison of face or feature can be drawn or conjectured. But pride and ambition were the spurs of both. Both were in arms for the omnipotence of the human mind. We may be sure Marlowe would have subscribed to Chatterton's words : 'God has sent His creatures into the world with arms long enough to reach anything if they chose to be at the trouble.'

He was, it appears, sparing in diet, lest he should 'make himself more stupid than God had made him,' and a contemporary record describes him as prepossessing in manner, with a proud air and remarkable eyes, piercing hawk's eyes, through which 'one could see his soul.'

It is not my purpose to recall the Rowley controversy, to discuss the methods or morality of Chatterton in his attempt to gain the ear of his times. He succeeded in drawing attention to his own works by ascribing them to a fifteenth-century author. We may condemn or forgive the falsehood. His extreme youth, his continuous ill-luck, his affection for his mother and sister, the pathos of his life, its early and tragic conclusion, are circumstances which soften our hearts and disarm our censures. Permit me to avoid the moral issue and to recount the salient facts of his career.

It chanced that in the muniment room of St. Mary Redcliffe there stood a number of chests, containing old deeds and documents, one of which was known as Master Canynge's coffer. Of these papers, considered valueless in that unantiquarian age, Chatterton's father was in the habit of making use to cover schoolbooks. It occurred to the boy that he might attribute his own compositions to Thomas Rowley, an imaginary friend of the famous Canynge, a wealthy Bristol merchant. Canynge was undoubtedly an historical character, a generous benefactor to his native city, who had been four times its Mayor in the reigns of Henry VI and Edward IV. Of St. Mary Redcliffe he was the reputed founder. Chatterton, however, invested him with imaginary qualities, invented for him a circle of friends, and made him a patron of art and letters. If poetry be, as Bacon called it, ' feigned history,' here you have it. St. Mary Redcliffe came to life. It ceased to be a mere building, a pile of stones. It embodied the thoughts, desires, hopes and fears, the innumerable acts of men and days gone by. The boy had no access to the facts, but imagination supplied them. It is not the function of the poet, as Aristotle said, to relate what has actually happened, the particular, but what may happen, the higher truth, the universal. To support the legend Chatterton produced a number of documents, prepared by himself, descriptive of the doings of Canynge and his friends, an account of which had been kept, so ran his tale, by the priest, Thomas Rowley.

This was a sufficiently astonishing fiction to be advanced by a child scarcely in his teens, and made credible by copies in his own hand of alleged fifteenth-century manuscripts. It was, however, but the ground-plan of the imposing imaginative structure. He proceeded to write poems of a surprising excellence, some in a stanza of his own invention, in a dialect which purported to be the English of that time. Though there were sceptics the design proved successful. For long, indeed, scholars debated the authenticity of the Rowley poems as hotly as they debated the Ossian originals. Nor was the matter finally set at rest until the publication of his *Essay on the Rowley Poems* by Professor Skeat in 1891.

The story of this famous deception has its humours. When he was fourteen Chatterton played an ingenious practical joke upon a Bristol citizen named Burgum, a prosperous tradesman, ambitious of social standing. The young antiquarian announced his discovery, among the St. Mary Redcliffe papers, of a coat of arms belonging to the De Bergham family, which proved its connexion with a noble English house. This, to the extreme gratification of Burgum, he subsequently produced, painted in colours, together with a document tracing the descent of the family from the Norman Conquest, attested by references to the Roll of Battle Abbey, and other charters, some purely fanciful. For this find he was rewarded with five shillings, and later produced further papers, including a poem, *The Romaunte of the Cnyghte*, composed, he said, about 1320 by John de Bergham, an accomplished gentleman well known in his own day. Thus suiting himself to local requirements the boy produced a number of documents and poems, in the fabrication of which he had no assistance save what he gathered from books and one or two dictionaries. To a local antiquarian, anxious to write the city's history, he supplied topographical material, described the ancient streets and walls, building within them churches and palaces to his pleasure. In 1768 the existing Gothic bridge over the river was replaced by a new structure, and

Chatterton invented an account of the ceremonies at the opening of the old bridge, the Mayor's procession across it and the public festivities on the occasion. In the following year he wrote to Horace Walpole, well known as a patron of art and letters, interested in antiquities. To attract Walpole's attention, Chatterton forwarded with his letter a document which he described as a copy of a fifteenth-century manuscript, *The Ryse of Peyncteyne yn Englande wroten by T. Rowleie, 1469, for Master Canynge.* Walpole wrote an encouraging reply, and Chatterton was emboldened to tell him of his circumstances, ' that he was the son of a poor widow, who supported him with great difficulty,' that he was apprenticed to an attorney, but anxious to find some congenial post which would enable him to pursue his favourite studies. Accompanying the letter was another manuscript entitled *Historie of Peyncters yn Englande bie T. Rowley.* Walpole's suspicions were aroused, and he sent the manuscript to Gray and Mason, who pronounced them forgeries. Walpole thereupon wrote again to Chatterton, advising him to continue in his profession until he had made a fortune sufficient to support him in following his natural inclinations. At this time Chatterton was about sixteen and a pretty regular contributor to one or two journals. In 1770 he decided to try his fortune in London. For three months he kept up a desperate struggle to earn his living, but in the end, too independent to seek assistance, and having passed several days without food, he tore up his papers and took a dose of arsenic. Thus, at seventeen, three months short of his eighteenth birthday, the proud, indignant soul hurried down to the shades.

Before leaving Bristol Chatterton left upon his desk a strange paper, described as *The Last Will and Testament of me, Thomas Chatterton, of the city of Bristol,* which, in a vein of sarcastic irony, disposed of his mental possessions. He had no others. Here are some of the items :

' I give and bequeath unto the Rev. Mr. J. Camplin, senior, all my humility. To Mr. Burgum all my prosody and gram-

mar . . . I leave also my religion to Dr. Cutts Barton,
Dean of Bristol . . . I leave my moderation to the politicians on both sides of the question. I leave my generosity
to the Right Worshipful Mayor, Thomas Harris, Esq. I
give my abstinence to the Sheriff's annual feast in general,
more particularly the Aldermen. Item, I give and bequeath
to Mr. William Mease a mourning ring with this motto,
"Alas, poor Chatterton!" provided he pays for it himself.
I leave the young ladies all the letters they have had from
me, assuring them they may be under no apprehensions from
the appearance of my ghost, for I die for none of them . . .
I leave my mother and sister to the protection of my friends,
if I have any."

This paper was the fruit of much bitter brooding, for it was
endorsed—'all this wrote between eleven and two o'clock,
Saturday, in the utmost distress of mind, April 14, 1770.'

The appearance of Chatterton, a poet inspired by the past,
and especially by the architecture of the past, a great mediæval
building—the appearance of such a poet in the age of prose
and reason, which despised the Gothic past, has in it something
surprising, something unexpected and instructive. The eighteenth century has had its admirers, and I find myself among its
admirers. It produced many of our noblest and most representative thinkers. It had abundance of good sense. It was
wonderfully wide-awake and clear-sighted. It was philosophical
and eloquent. It was wise and witty. Why then did Gray,
to our surprise, speak of it as 'this benighted age?' Why did
Arnold in the last century say of it, 'a kind of spiritual east wind
was at that time blowing?' The answer is that poetry, whatever poetry may be, could not flourish there. The atmosphere
was unfriendly. Is there, then, an antagonism between the
spirit of poetry and the spirit of reason, an irreconcilable feud?
Must we make a choice between them? It is a common
opinion. Hume thought the imagination the greatest enemy
of the reason. Macaulay argued that enlightenment and poetry

never go hand in hand, that as civilization advances poetry almost of necessity declines. Peacock goes further. Whether in earnest or in jest he declared that a poet is ' a semi-barbarian in a civilized community.' These are heavy tidings. And it can hardly be denied that there is something in the nature of the insulated understanding seeking after the origins and causes of things, in its very aim and methods, in its cold, analytic gaze, which quenches emotion, tends to belittle the objects of its investigations and may even blunt the edge of human happiness. It has an unenthusiastic eye. With wonder and admiration it professes no concern. And where there is no room for wonder and admiration there is no room for poetry. But constituted as we are by nature, can we sacrifice them ? We are nature's children and in her hands. Would she have us make rationality our single aim, and fill our hearts with happiness when we attained it ?

To bring this matter to an issue let me revert to Gothic architecture, which so inspired Chatterton, and to the mediæval cathedral, its most satisfying representative. Whatever else it be, if poetry can be written in stone, it is poetry. Or rather, there, as nowhere else in the world, will you find all the arts blended in a single harmonious whole. Within the noblest building he had ever known the mediæval man found in alliance, subtly intertwined, painting and sculpture and music, the best work of the greatest masters of the time. In this, at least, he was more fortunate than we, who for all our enlightenment have been unable to devise any such harmony, any such consummate union of the arts. A great disruption has taken place. With us, each is isolated, separated from the rest. For our music we must go to a concert hall, for our enjoyment of pictures to a gallery, for our poetry to the pages of a book. Let it stand, then, the Gothic cathedral, and it may well stand, as a symbol of poetic thought in all its manifestations. What did the men of the eighteenth century, of the age of prose and reason, make of it ? As might be expected, they could make nothing. They stood before the work of these architects, of which Blake thought the world had not been worthy, in complete bewilderment. The great minsters and abbeys were masterpieces in grotesque. To what purpose these eccentric structures, this extravagance and complexity of device and design ? How remote from the needs and necessities of life. How irreducible to the principles of reason and good sense. 'What unhappily remains to us of the architecture and sculpture of the time,' wrote Voltaire, ' is a fantastic compound of rudeness and filigree.' 'You know by reputation the Palace of St. Mark's,' said one of his fellow-countrymen, 'it is an ugly old fellow if ever there was one, massive, sombre and Gothic, in the most execrable taste.' And on the Baptistry at Florence, whose doors Michael Angelo thought beautiful enough to be the doors of Paradise, his comment was, 'a little less abominable than the Cathedral of St. Mark.'

'Let any one reflect,' remarks Addison in the *Spectator*, ' on the disposition of mind he finds in himself at his first entry into the Pantheon of Rome, and how his imagination is filled with something great and amazing ; and at the same time consider how little he is affected with the inside of a Gothic Cathedral, though it be five times larger than the other ; which can only arise from nothing else but greatness of manner in the one and meanness in the other.'

And again, 'a monstrous fabric, built after the Gothic manner and covered with innumerable devices in that barbarous kind of sculpture.' O Reason !—may we not cry ?—what follies are uttered in thy name ! These are not the judgements of stupid men, but on the contrary, men of the highest intelligence. They are the judgements of men, who desired above all things to understand, brought face to face with history and humanity, with the incomprehensible. Against the incomprehensible, reason revolts, but while we live I fear we shall have to put up with it. Logic is the best of keys to a logical structure, but where is the logic in the tangle history presents of ambitions, and hopes, and hates and fears, or that poetry presents in its admirations, and affections, and passion for beauty ? And how do you propose to interpret by means of it, to reduce to its concepts the great mediæval church, which *is* history and which *is* poetry ?

It embodies the ideals and aspirations of centuries. Its builders thought in high terms. It is pride and splendour. It is passion and desire. It rejoices the simple beholder. But it flings a constant challenge to the intellect. These heights and distances, these vistas and perspectives, these ascents from nave to chancel, and chancel to choir, these columns and transepts and galleries, these vaultings and painted windows, carved screens and shrines, these glooms and glories, tolling bells, chanting voices, these monuments and memorials of famous men and famous doings, this extraordinary coinage of the brain, what precisely are its rational values, and what system or science will elucidate them to us ? Can you prove it anything but a magnificent inutility, a superb aimlessness ? Is all this in the name of common sense to be rejected ? It speaks, and its speech is eloquent, but to Voltaire and Addison the speech was an unintelligible jargon, evidence of the mind in delirium.

We have become aware that somehow these judgements were mistaken, that Lincoln, and Durham and Westminster Abbey are not wholly absurd, or insipid, or vulgar, or lamentable. Whatever we think, at least we no longer say such things. They are no longer fashionable. But does the matter really end there ? If we were honest with ourselves perhaps we should say them, and declare poetry incompatible with intellectual enlightenment. Walpole called Dante ' a Methodist parson in Bedlam.' Voltaire spoke of the *Divine Comedy* as a ' monster.' Newton thought poetry ' a kind of ingenious nonsense.' Bentham declared it ' sheer misrepresentation ' and asserted that ' the quantity of pleasure being equal, push-pin was as good as poetry.' Even the divine Plato appears to have been in some

E

doubt. In his devotion to reason he felt called upon to expel the poets from his ideal commonwealth. ' I have a strong sense,' said Arnold, speaking of the Middle Ages, ' of the irrationality of that period, and the utter folly of those who take it seriously, and play at restoring it . . . Still it has practically the greatest charm and refreshment possible for me . . . There is something magical about it.' Strange words. Charm and the greatest possible refreshment are associated with irrationality !

What meets us here is the clash, the everlasting conflict between two orders of thought, both natural, both legitimate, the thought which proceeds by way of concept and idea, and the thought which takes another route, the way of myth and symbol and image. It meets us in every generation, in every culture, in every educated man of our own time. There is a double mind in us. We desire logic and we desire beauty. The intellect, with its sublime belief in itself, its own aspirations, its own assumptions, with its admirable determination to explore to the end and leave no irreducible remainder, how should it not be at war with poetry, which speaks a different, and for the reason a totally unintelligible language ? To the understanding, everything presents itself as a problem. To our own enlightened times life appears as a kind of examination paper of formidable questions, which it is the chief business of our existence to solve. We are presented with them, not in our works of science only, but in our novels and dramas. A dish of problems is served to us each morning by the thoughtful press. We sup full of problems. Intellectualism is in our life blood. Well, I, for one, am not prepared to abandon the pursuit of reason. I will endeavour to follow whithersoever the argument leads. So far as in me lies, I will endeavour to understand. Defeated, I will return to the assault, and again defeated, again return to it. I will employ every power of whatever intellect I possess. But I will not surrender my soul into its keeping. Not even at its command, though beauty elude its measurements, will I reject beauty, nor convert into a torturing problem the happiness I derive from Shakespeare, or Bach, or Raphael. I find them not less convincing than Euclid or Newton. Intellectualism is in our blood. Yes, but admiration is also in our blood. The language of poetry cannot be translated into the language of mathematics, nor that of beauty into the language of logic. Let us be content. Certainly neither language is sufficient for the interpretation of the world, since both are inadequate. 'There is in nature,' said Goethe, and he might have added 'in human nature,' 'an accessible and an inaccessible.' We begin, I believe, to perceive it. Our own understanding age is not too sure of its intellectual foundations. Reason looks nervously at her concepts, and science examines with some uneasiness her time-honoured axioms. It is whispered that 'the solution of the riddle of life in space and time lies outside space and time.' This is ancient doctrine. The mind returns upon itself. If it be accepted, perhaps we have here the beginnings of a reconciliation between reason and poetry.

English and Scottish Ballads [1]

There is a pleasant scene in the 'Winter's Tale' which introduces that light-fingered but delightful rascal Autolycus, offering, among his pedlar's wares, ballads for sale :

'O Master,' cries the servant who announces him, 'O Master, if you did but hear the pedlar at the door, you would never dance again after a tabor and pipe ; no, the bagpipe could not move you ; he sings several tunes faster than you'll tell money ; he utters them as he had eaten ballads, and all men's ears grow to his tunes.'

A little later we have the remark from Mopsa, 'I love a ballad in print a'-life, for then we are sure they are true.' Autolycus not only offers ballads for sale, but sings them too— 'I can bear my part, you must know, 'tis my occupation.' But Autolycus lived too late to reap the full glory of his profession. With the advent of printing the professional minstrel is shorn of much of his earlier importance and dignity ; he is no longer the only source of popular poetry. In this country, as soon as printing became common, the well-known songs and ballads were printed on broadsheets, and hawked through the country, as is described in the play quoted above. But in the train of printing came disrepute ; the broadsides were not confined to ballads ; satirical poems, attacks in verse upon institutions and individuals, were disseminated through the country in the same fashion. The genuine old songs, thus falling into bad company, were held by the cultivated in great contempt, until in Elizabethan times the term 'ballad' ceased

[1] An essay in *The Quarterly Review* on *The English and Scottish Popular Ballads*, edited by Francis James Child (5 vols., Boston, 1882–98) and *Old English Ballads*, selected and edited by Francis B. Gummere (Boston, 1894).

to be any recommendation in itself and came to be applied in an indiscriminate fashion to any poem which appealed to the crowd. The Puritans regarded the ballad with profound dislike as a source of social corruption ; ' scarcely a cat can look out of a gutter,' it was said, '. . . but presently a proper new ballad of a strange sight is indited.' The result of the disrepute into which the whole family of popular poems fell was that in 1648 ' ballad singers were suppressed, along with stage plays.' From that date until the publication of Percy's *Reliques* in 1765 only a discriminating critic here and there gave a thought to the poetry of the people or ventured to speak a word in its favour. The history of critical appreciation of the ballad before the era of the Romantic Revival contains indeed names few but honourable. That Shakespeare was thoroughly acquainted with the poetry of the people we know. How frequently and with what admirable effect the burden of a ballad or a snatch of popular song is introduced into the plays ! Ben Jonson was accustomed to say of the ballad of ' Chevy Chace ' that he would rather have been the author of it than of all his own works ; and Sir Philip Sidney, in his *Defence of Poesy*, speaks eloquently of the same piece ; ' Certainly I must confess my own barbarousness ; I never heard the old song of " Percy and Douglas " that I found not my heart moved more than with a trumpet.' But the people's poetry had long to wait for any further critical appreciation, though in the reign of James I some collections of ballads seem to have been made, under the title of ' Garlands.' We have, however, the authority of Addison for Dryden's admiration of the ballad :

> ' I have heard,' he remarks in No. 85 of the *Spectator*, ' that the late Lord Dorset, who had the greatest wit tempered with the greatest candour, and was one of the finest critics as well as one of the best poets of his age, had a numerous collection of old English ballads, and took a particular pleasure in the reading of them. I can affirm the same of

Mr. Dryden, and know several of the most refined writers of our present age who are of the same humour.' [1]

In this same number of the *Spectator* Addison gives an entertaining account of his own interest in ballad poetry :

'My humour of prying into all sorts of writing gives me,' he wrote, 'a great deal of employment when I enter any house in the country ; for I cannot for my heart leave a room before I have thoroughly studied the walls of it, and examined the several printed papers which are usually pasted upon them. The last piece that I met with upon this occasion gave me most exquisite pleasure. My reader will think I am not serious when I acquaint him that the piece I am going to speak of was the old ballad of the " Two Children in the Wood," which is one of the darling songs of the common people. This song,' he continues, 'is a plain simple copy of nature, and destitute of the helps and ornaments of art . . . There is even a despicable simplicity in the verse, and yet, because the sentiments appear genuine and unaffected, they are able to move the mind of the most polite reader with inward meltings of humanity and compassion. The incidents grow out of the subject, and are such as are the most proper to excite pity.'

Here and in the two papers which he devotes to a critical appreciation of ' Chevy Chace,' [2] Addison touches the points of real excellence in primitive and popular poetry. He praises the sentiments, as he calls them, in the ballad of ' Chevy Chace ' as ' extremely natural and poetical and full of the majestic simplicity which we admire in the greatest of the ancient poets.' Criticism such as this is noteworthy, because it displays an unusual insight into the true nature of poetry at a time when the ideals of art were narrowed by the influence of the English

[1] Dryden printed ' Chevy Chace,' ' Johnny Armstrong,' and other ballads in his *Miscellany Poems*, 1684.
[2] Nos. 70 and 74 of the *Spectator*. Johnson produced a counterblast to these papers in No. 177 of the *Rambler*.

classical school. It was to be expected that the representative of polite literature in the eighteenth century should protect himself against the sneers of the cultivated, and Addison adds : ' I must caution the reader not to let the simplicity of the style, which one may well pardon in so old a poet, prejudice him against the greatness of the thought.' Addison died in 1719, and in 1723 appeared the earliest printed collection of English ballads, by an editor whose name is unknown—perhaps Ambrose Philips, who was apparently inspired by the praise bestowed by the *Spectator* on ' Chevy Chace.' But this collection, though it attained some popularity, is of little account in literary history. We now approach the period, however, in which an interest in ancient popular poetry was to prove one of the main sources of a revolution in taste which supplied a fresh impulse and a fresh inspiration to the writers of the time. In 1724 Allan Ramsay published two miscellanies, *The Tea-Table Miscellany* and *The Evergreen*. The former was a collection of songs, some of them his own, and others drawn from various sources, but the book contained in addition some fine ballads. The latter collection was a more serious attempt to revive interest in old English poetry, and seems to have fallen comparatively flat in consequence. In 1760 Edward Capell published a book entitled *Prolusions ; or, Select Pieces of Ancient Poetry*, where appeared for the first time the true version of ' The Nut-Brown Mayde,' and in 1765 John Bowle published *Miscellaneous Pieces of Antient English Poetry*. These publications, though no single one of them can strictly be entitled a ballad collection, prove that there were signs of a revival of public taste for the old popular stories in verse, and, if we place beside them the opinion of the poet Gray in respect of the art which some of these old poems displayed, we shall be prepared for the chorus of applause, critical and uncritical, which greeted the publication in 1765 of the *Reliques of Ancient English Poetry* by Thomas Percy, after- wards Lord Bishop of Dromore. In a letter to Mason, Gray writes :

'I have got the old Scotch ballad on which "Douglas"[1]
was founded ['Child Maurice.'] . . . Aristotle's best rules
are observed in it in a manner that shews the author had
never read Aristotle. It begins in the fifth act of the play ;
you may read it two-thirds through without guessing what
it is about ; and yet, when you come to the end, it is impossible not to understand the whole story.'

Percy's *Reliques* has, of course, long been regarded as one of
the landmarks of English literary history. It cannot be said
that it absolutely created the taste for the qualities of the poetry
which it presented, but its appearance gives the date to the
rising of the new tide in literary taste. Long before the year
in which the *Reliques* appeared Percy stumbled upon a MS.,
'a scrubby shabby paper' volume, 'lying dirty on the floor
under the bureau in ye parlour' of the house of a certain
Humphrey Pitt of Shiffnal. Pitt's servants had been in the
habit of tearing out its leaves for the purpose of lighting the
fires. This folio MS. contained nearly two hundred poems,
songs, and metrical romances, and the handwriting proves that
it was probably written about 1650, or a hundred years before
its discovery by Percy, to whom it was given by Pitt.[2] It
contained compositions of all times and dates from the fourteenth century downwards, and was Percy's main source for
his printed collection. But while Percy drew upon the MS.,
it was not printed until the repeated requests made by Professor
Child and Dr. Furnival to the Bishop's descendants at length
resulted in the publication (1867–8) of the secret source of
Percy's wealth. The result of the publication was to add
nothing to the gratitude due to the editor of the *Reliques*. His
tone in commending the book to the public had been modest
and even apologetic, and, in order to find favour with the

[1] Home's tragedy.

[2] Pitt informed Percy that the MS. had been found in a library of old
books which was thought to have belonged to a lawyer, Thomas Blount,
author of the *Ancient Tenures*, 1679 ; *Law Dictionary*, 1671, and other
works.

polite reader, he had added some modern poems, 'to atone,' as he remarked, 'for the rudeness of the more obsolete poems,' and, 'to take off from the tediousness of the longer narratives, intermingled little elegant pieces of the lyric kind.' But, as editor, Percy took an astonishingly liberal view of an editor's privileges, altering, adding to, and amending the poems without hesitation and without scruple :

'As to the text, he looked on it as a young woman from the country with unkempt locks, whom he had to fit for fashionable society. . . . All fashionable requirements Percy supplied. He puffed out the thirty-nine lines of the " Child of Ell " to two hundred : he pomatumed the " Heir of Lin " till it shone again ; he stuffed bits of wool into " Sir Cawline," " Sir Aldingar " ; he powdered everything. The desired result was produced ; his young woman was accepted by Polite Society, taken to the bosom of a Countess, and rewarded her *chaperon* with a mitre.'

Beside the folio MS. the other sources upon which Percy drew were some minor MS. collections, Scottish ballads supplied to him by Sir David Dalrymple, the printed broadsides, and a few old printed collections. What Percy had done for English ballads Walter Scott did for the popular poetry of his own country. In 1802 appeared his *Minstrelsy of the Scottish Border*, one of the finest collections ever made, the result of 'ballad forays' into Liddesdale for direct oral versions of the well-known legends. Among other collections may be mentioned Ritson's in 1792 (*Ancient Songs*), Jamieson's in 1806, and Motherwell's in 1827. All are now superseded by Child's great critical edition, a treasury of popular poetry which takes classic rank.

The charm of the authentic ballad probably consists in this, that we have here poetry reduced to its simplest elements. The qualities of the greater part of modern poetry are appreciable only by persons who have had some æsthetic cultivation, who have learned to like it. Thus it is that, as Bagehot said, ' with the great majority of people a faith in poetry struggles to be extricated, but it is not extricated.' The untrained ear will appreciate a simple melody, but to enjoy Wagner demands some musical culture.

' When people tell me,' says Emerson, ' they do not relish poetry, and bring me Shelley, or Aikin's Poets, or I know not what volumes of rhymed English, to show that it has no charm, I am quite of their mind. But this dislike of the *books* only proved their liking of poetry. For they relish Æsop, cannot forget him or not use him ; bring them Homer's " Iliad," and they like that ; or the " Cid," and that rings well ; read to them from Chaucer, and they reckon him an honest fellow. . . . Give them Robin Hood's ballads, or " Griselda," or " Sir Andrew Barton," or " Sir Patrick Spens," or " Chevy Chase," and they like these well enough. . . . They like poetry without knowing it as such.'

Ballad poetry, then, is poetry that needs for its appreciation no technical knowledge, no atmosphere of culture, no superfine taste ; it needs only an interest in human life and the world of men and women. The ballads of ' Chevy Chace,' of ' Fair Rosamond,' of ' Robin Hood,' introduce us to this world of intensely real emotions such as can be read on men's faces, and need no subtle psychological skill to analyse or detect them. To compare an authentic ballad with a characteristic modern poem is to bring together the poles of the poetic world. To modern poetry belongs the personal note, the note of the individual who produces it ; the poetry of Tennyson or of Arnold is suffused with Tennyson or Arnold ; it is individual and personal throughout. Again to modern poetry belongs the note of subjectivity : much of its interest is derived from the ideas and sentiments abroad in it ; it is usually the distillation of a mood of thought ; it suggests more than it relates —in a word the self-conscious artist overshadows it. But the ballad tells a straightforward story and means no more than it says. It is not subjective, distilled from the mind, but objective, an account of actual occurrences, and its interest is resident entirely in things and persons instead of in sentiments and ideas, in what has happened rather than in what has been felt and thought. It bears no trace of the individual artist, but is a disinterested impersonal presentation of something that has actually taken place. Primitive poetry thinks only of what is said, the poetry of culture much of how it is said. In the admirable introduction to his *Old English Ballads*, a book in which the rare combination of sound scholarship and fine literary feeling is unusually conspicuous, Professor Gummere in a brief sentence sums up these points of dissimilarity. ' Instead of the poet's mood, the poet's sensations and manner, we have the mood, sensations, and manner of the *object* which called out the ballad.'

It is not difficult to account for these differences. It may be said in the first place that ballads proper can hardly be accurately described as belonging to literature, in the strict sense of the word. They were not written, for they were produced at a period when it is not possible to divide the individuals that compose the race into ' lettered' and ' unlettered' classes. They are the poetry of a people unacquainted with writing, not to speak of printing. They are poems which we owe to oral tradition, which, although we possess them in a printed form, existed for generations only in the minds of individuals, were stored in the only library known to their authors, the library of memory. The earliest ballads, as the derivation of the word implies, were no doubt songs accompanying a dance, and it is not permissible to draw any distinction between the song and the ballad, the lyrical and the narrative poem. Both were intended to be sung, were produced for singing purposes. Sidney speaks of ' the *olde song* of Percy and Douglas.' But the early ballad besides being a song was in some respects a drama, and it seems probable that the dance for which it supplied the music was in some cases of a simple dramatic character. Studied scientifically, ballads yield much interesting information as contemporary documents ; studied comparatively, they reveal the fact that the same or similar plots and incidents are common to the ballads of all the countries of Europe. Nothing can be more remarkable than 'the sameness of tone, of incident, of legend, of primitive poetical formulæ in the ballads of Scotland, France, Provence, Portugal, Italy, Greece.'—'They are,' says Andrew Lang, 'the immemorial inheritance at least of all European peoples.' In this respect they may be most fitly compared to *Märchen*, the nursery tales which are the common possession of many races. The question of the relation of the ballad to the epic opens up a wide field of speculation, but whatever hypothesis be adopted, for practical purposes the ballad proper may be regarded as a miniature epic. Both belong to the period of unwritten poetry. As Gummere says, 'with the spread of letters among the people, this poetry of the unlettered passed away ; the revival of learning, the secularization of art, brought in their train the lapse of impersonal and objective poetry, and the rise of the confidential and sentimental poet.' In England, as in all other countries, prose composition had to wait for the writer, the pen-man, but, before prose was created, poetry was universal. It lived, as Herder said, 'in the ears of the people ; it was the flower of a nation's character, language, and country, of its occupations, its prejudices, its aspirations, and its soul.' The authentic ballad, then, because it makes appeal to the simple human feelings, and ignores the distinction between people of artistic culture and people of no culture at all, because the qualities of the ballad are such qualities as are appreciable by any member of the great human family—for these reasons the authentic ballad is the only popular poetry. There is no other popular poetry save this that springs spontaneously from the life and heart of unlettered humanity. And its characteristics are such as might be expected in an art product not laboured and schooled into subjection to rules of art. It employs assonance frequently in place of rhyme :

> 'But at Sir Andrew he shot then ;
>> He made sure to hit his *marke* ;
>> Under the spole of his right arm
>> He smote Sir Andrew through the *heart*,'

or—

> 'Haf owre, haf owre to Aberdour :
>> It's fiftie fadom *deip* :
>> And thair lies guid Sir Patrick Spens
>> Wi' the Scots lords at his *feit*.'

It enters without introduction upon the subject ; its style is the plain business-like style, direct and straightforward. The 'Banks of Yarrow' opens with a stanza singularly compressed :

> 'Late at een, drinking the wine
>> And ere they paid the lawing,
>> They set a combat them between
>> To fight it in the dawing.'

It would be difficult to enter more immediately upon the story than here or in the ballad of 'Childe Waters' :

> 'Childe Watters in his stable stoode,
>> And stroaket his milk-white steede ;
>> To him came a faire young ladye
>> As ere did weare woman's weede.'

But perhaps no better example of the brusque manner of the ballad can be adduced than the opening verses of 'The Demon Lover.' What a tragedy in little these stanzas present.

> '"O where have you been, my long, long love,
>> This long seven years and more ?"
>> "O I'm come to seek my former vows
>> Ye granted me before."

> '"O hold your tongue of your former vows,
>> For they will breed sad strife ;
>> O hold your tongue of your former vows,
>> For I am become a wife."'

Then, again, recurring phrases are very characteristic of popular poetry ; as in Homer, textual repetition is frequent :

> ' They hadna sailed a league, a league,
> A league, but barely three,'

or—

> ' He hadna gone a step, a step,
> A step, but barely one.'

The ballad usually reproduces in full the words of a speech when reported, exactly as in Homer. Such recurring phrases, as Gummere says, make for the communal character of the ballad ; an artist, on the other hand, avoids commonplaces and seeks to vindicate his own self. As in Homer also, recurring epithets are of the very essence of the style of these old poems. As Achilles is ' swift-footed ' so Robin Hood is ' bold,' and such phrases as ' the comely King,' ' the bluid-red wine,' ' a berry-brown steed,' take us back to the poetry of ' the rosy-fingered dawn,' ' the wine-coloured sea,' ' the far-darting Apollo.'

But the similes of the English and Scottish ballads are neither so numerous nor so sustained as those of Homer. They are indeed comparatively rare and, in marked contrast to the long-drawn-out comparisons in the ' Iliad ' or ' Odyssey,' rarely extend beyond a single line :

> ' When this letter came Jonnë until,
> His heart was as blyth as birds on the tree ;
> " Never was I sent for before any king,
> My father, my grandfather, nor none but me." '

> ' " Sweavens are swift, master," quoth John,
> " As the wind that blows o'er a hill ;
> For if it be never soe lowde this night,
> To-morrow it may be still." '

No less characteristic is the employment of the numbers three, seven, twenty-four, and thirty-three :

> ' A better shot in mery Caerlel
> This seven year was not seen.'

> ' And Scarlette he was flying afoote,
> Fast over stock and stone,
> For the sheriffe with seven-score men
> Fast after him is gone.'

> ' There came three wooers out of the west,
> Booted and spurred as ye well might see.'

The ballad of the people rejoices, too, in the precious metals.
' Blood,' said Charles Lamb, ' is made as light of in our early
tragedies as money in a modern sentimental comedy.' The
genuine ballad scatters gold and silver in magnificent profusion :

> ' And every arrow an ellë long,
> With pecock well idyght,
> Inocked all with whyte silver ;
> It was a seemly sight.'

> ' A grete courser with sadle and brydil
> With gold burnisht full bright.'

> ' She set her foot upon the ship,
> No mariners could she behold,
> But the sails were o' the taffetie,
> And the masts o' the beaten gold.'

Gummere lays it down that all our English and Scottish
ballads are in the form of a rhymed stanza. The stanza may
be a couplet, or it may be a four-line stanza, of which the
usual, though not invariable, type is one in which the second
and fourth lines rhyme together, as here, for example :

> ' Ye Highlands and ye Lowlands
> Oh, where have you been ?
> They have slain the Earl of Murray,
> And they layd him on the green.'

But we must note as one of the characteristics of all ballad poetry its great licence, a licence which may be exhibited in the number of syllables in the line, or in the matter of the rhyming scheme. Occasionally the four lines of the stanza are exchanged for six, a kind of overflow which may be managed with considerable effect. How admirably it is introduced by Rossetti in his ballad of ' The King's Tragedy,' to heighten the emphasis of an important stanza :

> ' Quoth the King : " Thou speak'st but for one Estate,
>   Nor doth it avow thy gage.
> Let my liege lords hale this traitor hence ! "
>   The Graeme fired dark with rage :—
> " Who works for lesser men than himself,
>   He earns but a witless wage." '

The metrical laxities and the occasional looseness of construction in primitive poetry are the natural outcome of an ' imperfect artistic control,' and may be said to belong to the period of its production, to be the appropriate manner of poems marked by spontaneity and simplicity of style, an index to the objective character, the naïve unconscious art they may be expected to display.

' The prevailing view,' says Gummere, ' is that the metrical scheme came from the Latin hymns of the Church, and the irregularities of practice from influence of older native verse, but there are difficulties even in this simple assumption. There is a possibility that these popular metres, like the refrain, which come out of the Church to the people, had previously gone out of the people into the Church, and we may thus think of a continuity in metre from older ballads.'

In respect of rhyme, it may be said, despite Milton's famous dictum that ' rime was the invention of a barbarous age to set off wretched matter and lame metre,' that it is as ancient as poetry itself, and a feature of all ballad poetry with which we are familiar. In English ballads rhyme is the basis of the whole musical scheme, though alliteration and assonance have their place in it.

The movement of the verse in our primitive poetry is almost invariably iambic, though movements other than iambic are not unknown, as, for example :

> ' Hie upon Hielands
> And laigh upon Tay,
> Bonnie George Campell
> Rode out on a day,'

or—

> ' O where hae you been, Lord Randal, my son ? '

or—

> ' O where hae you ridden this lee lang day ?
> O where hae you stolen this lady away ? '

or—

> ' Seynt Stevene was a clerk in Kyng Herowde's halle,
> And served him of bred and cloth, as every Kyng befalle.'

The features just mentioned may be taken as common to all our ballad poetry, and many of them common to the ballad poetry of other countries no less. And it is out of this fact that the most difficult problem with which the student of popular poetry is called upon to deal, the problem of authorship, arises.

' If,' writes Gummere, ' the chief characteristics of a ballad are those which belong to the product of a community rather than to the work of an artist, and so force us to abandon certain ideas inseparable from recent poetry, how far are we to go in this surrender of the modern standard, and in what degree shall we hold the community responsible for the actual making of the ballad ? Where, if at all, are we to admit an individual poet in the process ? '

Herder may stand as representative of the critics who regard

F

ballad poetry as composed in a real sense by the community, by the people, and not by individual makers. He looked upon it as the product of a stage in a people's history in which there existed perfect homogeneity, a complete sympathy, among the individual units who composed the race, and of a stage in which improvisation, singing, dancing, music, and song were products of the communal life as natural as are the ' profuse strains ' of the skylark's ' unpremeditated art.' In short, the community itself was the unit, itself the individual that composed its songs. To the objection that it is inconceivable that a community can produce poetry, it may be replied : How did the community produce speech, language, or are these, too, the work of the individual ? What of social custom, what of religion, what of law ? This theory, then, suggests that, at a certain stage in a people's history, a well-known story might easily take on rhythmic form, partly because the rhythmic is a more intense and emphatic form, and thus the more easily carried in the memory and handed on by oral tradition. It is indisputable that the theory of community authorship would account for many of the characteristics of popular poetry ; it would account, for example, for the endless number of versions in which all popular songs survive. This theory looks upon the minstrels as professional singers of songs already in existence rather than their authors ; regards them as of later appearance in the field of history, when the community was losing its homogeneous character, and losing with it the power of improvisation. The decay of popular poetry begins with the professional singer, and is completed with the arrival upon the stage of the individual artist. Conscious art now displaces Nature, and popular poetry is no longer possible. The difficulty in accepting this theory of ballad-origins lies in the impossibility for us of re-creating in the imagination a condition of society in which unpremeditated spontaneous song flowed from a community. A work of art always suggests to us an artist, a poem suggests a poet, and the majority of modern critics lend little encouragement to the conception of communal authorship.

' So far,' says Courthope, ' from the ballad being a spontaneous product of popular imagination, it was a type of poem adapted by the professors of the declining art of minstrelsy from the romances once in favour with the educated classes. Everything in the ballad—matter, form, composition—is the work of the minstrel ; all that the people do is to remember and repeat what the minstrel has put together.'

But Courthope lays too much upon the minstrel, and the very simplicity of his explanation renders it unconvincing.[1] We are inclined to believe with Gummere that ' the ballad belonged to the people, and was the exclusive property of minstrels as little in the making as the singing.' Child's introduction would, no doubt, have dealt with the whole subject and resumed the evidence, but as it is we are left without any complete summary if we except the short but excellent study of the question by Gummere. It is clear, as he points out, that if we are to form a judgment of value upon so difficult a point we must first get rid of the modern notions of composition —methods of composition, that is—and modern ideas of literary property, the ownership of a poem by the man who makes it. We must try to imagine a state of society in which poetry was a common possession. ' Solitary composition would have been as difficult for primitive man to understand as communal authorship is hard for us.' In the ballad-making age, says Ten Brink, ' there was no production, there was only reproduction.' That is to say, there—

[1] Courthorpe, in pursuance of his thesis, instances the history of the well-known ballad of ' Mary Hamilton,' accepting Sharpe's theory that it was founded upon the story of a Mary Hamilton who was executed in Russia in 1719. But Lang (*Blackwood's Magazine*, 1895, Sept., pp. 381 ff.) has shown the extreme improbability of the truth of Sharpe's somewhat plausible theory.

' was a common stock of traditions, memories, experiences, held in common by large populations, in constant use on the lips of numberless persons, told and re-told in many forms with countless changes, variations and modifications ; without conscious artistic purpose, with no sense of personal control or possession, with no constructive aim either in plot or treatment, no composition, in the modern sense of the word. Such a mass of poetic material in the possession of a large community was, in a sense, *fluid*, and ran into a thousand forms almost without direction or premeditation.' [1]

Or, as Gummere puts it, ' all was in flux ; out of a common store of tradition, by a spontaneous and universal movement, song rose and fell according to the needs of the community.' ' Let us imagine,' says Ten Brink, ' an epoch where the same culture, the same sentiments, the same expressions, are the property of a whole community. . . . Imagine a poetry oscillating perpetually between reminiscence and improvisation.' Suggestions like these make demands upon the imagination to which the average man is probably not prepared to respond, but it may not be superfluous to remark that it is not contended that we possess in our ballad-books any perfect specimens of the primitive ballad whose origin is here described, the ballad as it fell hot from the lips of the community. In the words of Steinthal :

' Dip from the brook a pailful of water, and one has captured no brook ; write down a version of some folk-song, and it is no folk-song more. There is no stability about it : among Russians or Servians a song of eight or ten lines has endless variations. An Italian girl sang a song several times, but each time sang it with a difference : when asked the reason she said she could not help it, as the thing came to her so—*mi viene così*.' [2]

We do not possess, then, the primitive ballad of the people,

[1] H. W. Mabie, *A Book of Old English Ballads*.
[2] Gummere's Introduction, p. xxxvii.

and it may be asked of what value is speculation regarding the origin of something we do not possess. The reply is that in the ballad poetry which survives there is a suggestion of a poetry of which our ballads are but the fragmentary representatives. They exhibit qualities not altogether explicable by the fact of their oral transmission, but suggestive of a communal authorship. Let us say, then, that the history of the ballad begins with a simple chorus at a village festival in connexion with some event of general interest. Here and there the same event would produce under similar influences a memorable phrase or two which passed easily from mouth to mouth. On a similar occasion memory would play a part in recalling the simple chorus or the memorable phrase, to which others might be added, and a stanza or stanzas emerge. The gift of improvisation, it ought to be borne in mind, was and is no uncommon gift among peasant peoples. Their simpler thoughts and feelings run to musical words more easily than the thoughts and feelings of individuals who belong to civilized societies. Civilization restrains the expression of natural feeling, and introduces into speech the artificial and conventional. Nor did the improviser compose verses at the command of his imagination ; the material already existed, the style and metre were fixed ; he was at once an adapter and an original poet. Among his material, lines and stanzas existed which suggested others, and in the end a certain unity of *motif* or idea would be attained. The primitive ballad, then, may best be described as a composite poem, a *cento*. But its history does not end here. Hitherto we have conceived the community as active, the actual maker of the poem.

Now enters the minstrel, the professional singer of the people's ballads. He chants the favourite songs, and is everywhere a welcome visitor. Gradually the people take on a passive character as audience : they appreciate the poem, but no longer participate in making or singing it. The professional singer also develops. From a passive singer of songs gathered from oral tradition, he becomes an active meddler or artist : adds to the poem he sings, and even makes others wholly new on similar models. As the artist becomes more and more prominent, the communal elements of the primitive poetry sink further and further out of sight, and before the era of printing is reached only the survivals of these elements remain to give a clue to the original character of the poems to which they belonged. 'We have a series of ballads made from the beginning of the fourteenth century down to the beginning of our own, but the Anglo-Saxon ballads are matter of inference.'

Adopting this view, then, we may say that the original composers of the primitive songs and ballads of these and other countries were not poets by profession who composed an original version. There never was an original version, since ballads are poems rather evolved than composed, and the inspiration that produced them did not belong to any single individual. The best version of a ballad, then, will not be necessarily the oldest ; the best version will be the best from a poetical standpoint, and we need make no search for the author's actual words. It will follow that a chronological study of a ballad is impossible, since the date of a true ballad is indeterminable. They are dateless poems, and because no single author produced these primitive songs, they are authorless also.

As is inevitable, all the ballads we possess exist in numerous versions, and it is to be observed that the later versions are frequently superior. We may account for this by saying that the more melodious or stronger or more striking stanzas would naturally be best remembered. The unconscious critical faculty at work through generations would preserve the best lines or passages of a version, and add to them the best taken from other versions, rejecting the feebler ones. It ought, however, to be added that with the advent of printing, and more particularly is this true of England, the oral versions suffered severely at the hands of printers and self-appointed editors. It not infrequently happened also that the version which first appeared in print was a weak version, but the effect of its distribution was to drive the better oral versions out of the field.

The resemblance among the ballads of the various European countries is very marked, and this wide distribution of similar topics argues a great antiquity for the poems which treat of them, and may fairly be regarded as constituting a serious difficulty in the way of the theory that ballads owe their origin to a class of professional minstrels. We have proof, too, that from the very earliest times the Germanic race made and sang ballads, and we know that, whatever these poems may have been like, our existing ballads are the lineal descendants of that older pre-historic poetry, which in its turn sprang centuries ago from the soil of countries other than our own, the soil of the ancestral home of the race. ' The Germanic ballad can be traced in Denmark, Norway, Sweden, Iceland, the Färöe Islands, Scotland, England, Netherlands, and Germany.'— ' Almost every Norwegian, Swedish or Icelandic ballad is found in a Danish version.' It would seem, therefore, that, while the ballads of each country possess certain private property in material—certain distinctive qualities—they possess other qualities and other material in common with all branches of the great Aryan family.

' There are certain incidents,' says Andrew Lang, ' like that of the return of the dead mother to her oppressed children ; like the sudden recovery of a fickle bridegroom's heart by the patient affection of his first love ; like the adventures of May Colvin with a lover who has slain seven women, and tries to slay her ; like the story of the bride that pretends to be dead, that she may escape from a detested marriage—which are in all European countries the theme of popular song.'

A part of the material is held in common, then, but we must also note differences. There is, for example, in the ballad poetry

of England and Scotland little of a mythical character, and in
this the primitive poetry of Germany resembles our own. But,
on the other hand, Norway and Sweden possess many ballads
in which the myth plays an important part. Our early poetry
too is deficient in the heroic lay, which Scandinavia produced
plentifully. In the same way the plot and situations of primitive
poetry are traceable in some cases to the same story-roots, but
exhibit modifications and variations in each country's ballads.
The Danish ballads have been arranged by one of their best
students in four classes : 1. Heroic ballads ; 2. Ballads of myth
and enchantment ; 3. Historic ballads ; 4. Ballads of chivalry.
If we compare these with the English and Scottish ballads in
Child's collection, we shall notice that we possess few or no
specimens of the first and second classes. Child's table is as
follows :

1. Romances of chivalry and legends of the popular history
   of England ;
2. Ballads involving various superstitions : as of fairies, elves,
   magic and ghosts ;
3. Tragic love-ballads ;
4. Other tragic ballads ;
5. Love-ballads not tragic.

Scott, in his *Minstrelsy of the Scottish Border*, divides the ballads
in his collection simply into—

1. Historical ballads ;
2. Romantic ballads ;
3. Imitations of these by modern authors.

But the poems which fall within the last division may be
left out of account in dealing with our primitive poetry. The
literary as opposed to the authentic ballad, just like the literary
as opposed to the authentic epic, possesses certain unmistakable
marks of sophistication. The ballad form has been revived
with success by many modern poets, and we have had attempts,
not a little interesting, to pour the wine of modern sentiment into the old bottles. But Rossetti's ' King's Tragedy '

differs from 'Sir Patrick Spens' as 'Paradise Lost' from the 'Iliad.'

The study of a ballad which may be classed under the title 'historical' reveals how little knowledge of origins can be gleaned even by careful investigation. Take the most important ballad-cycle which our literature contains, that of Robin Hood. The popularity of the Robin Hood ballads has been from the earliest recorded mention of them extreme, but while their hero has a niche secure in the heart and imagination of the nation, the historical basis for the story is quite indeterminable. 'A tale of Robyn Hood' is a very old proverb for an idle and untruthful story, but no mention of Robin in *literature* is made before the latter half of the reign of Edward III. No earlier notice of him has yet been recovered than the reference made by the author of 'Piers Plowman' (about 1362) to 'Rhymes of Robin Hood' as 'better known to idle fellows than pious songs.' The next reference is in Wyntoun's *Scottish Chronicle*, written about 1420, where Robin Hood and Little John are mentioned.

The first reference to Robin Hood as an *historical person* occurs in a passage of the *Scotichronicon*, a work partly written by Fordun, Canon of Aberdeen, between 1377 and 1384, and partly by his pupil Abbot Bower about 1450. Bower's part of the chronicle is very untrustworthy. He largely interpolated the work of his master, and sometimes with the absurdest fictions. Among these interpolations is to be found the first reference which can be spoken of as *historical* to Robin Hood.

'At this time [sc. 1266] from the number of those who had been deprived of their estates arose the celebrated bandit, Robin Hood [with little John and their accomplices], whose achievements the foolish vulgar delight to celebrate in comedies and tragedies, while the ballads upon his adventures sung by the jesters and minstrels are preferable to all others.'

It is particularly instructive to note, then, that the hero of the most popular cycle of English ballad poetry is never mentioned by any contemporary historian or chronicler, but is first heard of a hundred years after the latest date at which he can possibly be supposed to have lived.

'Robin Hood', as Child says, 'is absolutely the creation of the ballad muse. The earliest mention we have of him is as the subject of ballads. The only two early historians who speak of him, as a ballad hero, pretend to have no information about him except what they derive from ballads, and show that they have none other by the description they give of him ; this description being in entire conformity with ballads in our possession, one of which is found in a MS. as old as the older of these two writers.'

It may fairly be said that, if it prove impossible to trace so remarkable a cycle to its source, it is not to be expected that the origin of an ordinary unattached ballad will offer an easier problem. The study of an ancient ballad, too, frequently argues that, though it tells a story of which history gives the actual date, it suggests an antiquity of which it does not seem to speak. An ancient ballad, late in its life, may put on without much ado the garment of an historical story to which it bears a resemblance, and thus hide its own age under a veil of comparatively modern names and allusions.[1] There have been of course many more or less ingenious theories respecting the origin of Robin, Little John, the Friar, and Maid Marian : none of which can be said to appear convincing. Ritson connected the main personages with characters in the old morris-dances. Wright suggests that Robin Hood was 'one among the personages of the early mythology of the Teutonic people,' and a

---

[1] Cf. M. Arnold, *The Study of Celtic Literature*, p. 61 : 'The first thing that strikes one, in reading the "Mabinogion," is how evidently the mediæval story-teller is pillaging an antiquity of which he does not fully possess the secret : he is like a peasant building his hut on the site of Halicarnassus or Ephesus ; he builds, but what he builds is full of materials of which he knows not the history, or knows by a glimmering tradition merely ; stones, "not of this building," but of an older architecture, greater, cunninger, more majestical.'

German scholar, Kuhn, has endeavoured to prove that Robin is no other in name and substance than the god Woden. But the serious study of origins is not greatly advanced by such unsupported hypotheses. One point might perhaps be noted in passing. The title Earl of Huntingdon, occasionally found associated with Robin Hood, is without any ballad authority, and is derived from a late sixteenth-century play by Anthony Munday, in which Robin is represented as a nobleman in disguise, a conception due apparently to the dramatist's imagination.

If we turn from the scholastic aspects of the subject to consider the poetical qualities of popular poetry, we shall find ourselves more largely occupied with Scottish than with English ballads. Lang notices, and with justice, ' the comparative flatness and insipidity of the English ballad by the side of those belonging to other countries and dealing with the same subject.' —' The ballads of the Lowland Scotch,' he says, for example, ' have a fire which we miss in English popular poems,' and they omit ' the didactic drivel ' and prosaic incidents which spoil many of the English ballads we possess. Lang accounts for the comparative inferiority of the English ballad by reminding us that it is only in a few cases that they have been obtained by *oral tradition*, and much of the superfluous and commonplace in them may without hesitation be ascribed to the early editors and printers. Many of the Scottish ballads, on the other hand, were taken down from the lips of the people, and preserve therefore something of the freshness and vitality which in the case of the former were destroyed by the broadside versions. One is reminded, too, of the quotation made by Matthew Arnold, in his *Celtic Literature*, from an Irish poem in which the Saxon is described as ' dull and creeping ' :

> ' For acuteness and valour, the Greeks,
> For excessive pride, the Romans,
> For dulness, the creeping Saxons ;
> For beauty and amorousness, the Gaẹdhils.'—

and one is reminded also of his general thesis, his contention that to the Celtic element in English literature is due much of the turn displayed by its best writers for style and natural magic, and that the vein of piercing regret and stormy passion it contains is Celtic. The Celtic genius is probably best displayed in such short flights of poetry as the song and the ballad : it fails in architectural faculty, in the constructive power without which no great poem can be produced, in imaginative range and grasp, in what we may call the unifying imagination. Still another point might be noted in respect of the admitted inferiority of the English ballads : the influence of the landscape, the character of the country in which they were produced :

> ' If we look at the whole course of Border poetry,' says Veitch, ' we shall find that the scenery of the district in which it grew up has had a marked influence over it . . . The scenes of nearly all the most powerful and striking of the historical ballads are laid in the wilds around the heads of the Teviot and the Reed, and in the dark recesses of the mosses of the Tarras and the Liddel . . . It is also remarkable that the scenes of the most tragic and pathetic ballads and songs are to be found on the soft green braes of Yarrow, while the strains of the most tender of the love-songs first burst on the ear in the grassy and wooded haughs of the Tweed.'

Lang thinks that the inferiority of the English ballads is most marked among those dealing with supernatural subjects. To take an example : the Scottish ballad of ' Chevy Chace ' differs from the English by the introduction of a dream which in a singularly impressive and romantic fashion warns the Douglas of his approaching death :

> ' But I hae dreamed a weary dream
> Beyond the Isle of Sky,
> I saw a dead man win a fight,
> But I think that man was I.'

' The supernatural,' Lang contends, ' is almost invariably treated in a gross and flat style by the English balladist.'

Of the orthodox ornaments of poetry Spenser found the poetry of the Irish bards, to whom when in Ireland he listened, singularly destitute.

> ' I have caused diverse of them to be translated unto me that I might understand them ; and surely they savoured of sweete witt and good invention, but skilled not of the goodly ornaments of Poetrye ; yet were they sprinckled with some prety flowers of theyr owne naturall devise, which gave good grace and comliness unto them.'

We have already remarked that popular poetry deals very sparingly in simile, and it is noteworthy that even among the ballads of the North Country, over which the scenery of the district, as Veitch points out, had an unmistakably shaping influence, descriptions or allusions to landscape are very occasional. Occasional as they are, however, when they do occur in the Border ballads, they strike home by their penetrating truthfulness and simplicity, often in the flashing plainness of a single phrase. In the English ballads the references to scenery are somewhat commonplace :

' When shaws [woods] been sheene, and shradds [coppices] full
    faire
        And leaves both large and longe,
        It is mery, walking in the fair forest,
        To hear the small bird's song.'

But in a stanza like the following, which comes from a poem that had its birth among the Border hills, there is, as Veitch has pointed out, a wonderful force in the simple exactness of the concluding line :

      ' But he wasna on his berry-brown steed,
        Nor twa miles from the town,
      Till up it starts these three fierce men,
        Among the bent sae brown.'

Such a stanza flashes an instant picture upon the mind : we can see it as in life or on a canvas, the three fierce faces starting up in the rider's path among the long brown grass that clothes the barrenness of the Border hills.

Or take this description of the removal of the body of a lover secretly slain :

> ' Then she cried on her waiting maid,
>   Aye ready at her ca' :
> " There is a knight into my bower ;
>   'Tis time he were awa'."

> ' The ane has ta'en him by the head,
>   The other by the feet,
> And thrown him in the wan water,
>   That ran baith wide and deep.'

Everyone must feel that there is a singular appropriateness between the dread act here narrated and the scene suggested to the sense by the—

> ' wan water,
> That ran baith wide and deep.'

The popular poetry of the Border attains at times to the highest reaches of pathos and of power. We do not know that there is anywhere to be found in the whole range of narrative poetry a passage that can fairly be said to eclipse this from ' Edom o' Gordon ' (cited by Veitch), descriptive of the savage warfare of the old Border days. A tower is besieged and defended by a lady in the absence of her husband : Edom o' Gordon sets it on fire, and to save one of her children the valiant lady lowers her over the wall, trusting to the mercy of the besiegers for the child.

> ' They row'd her in a pair of sheets
>   And tow'd her owr the wa',
> But on the point of Edom's spear
>   She gat a deadly fa'.

' O bonny, bonny was her mouth,
    And chirry were her cheeks,
And clear, clear was hir yellow hair,
    Whereon the red bluid dreeps !

' Then wi' his speir he turn'd her owr ;
    O gin hir face was wan !
He said, " You are the first that e'er
    I wist alive again.

' " Busk and boon my merry men all,
    For ill dooms I do guess ;
I canna luik on that bonny face,
    As it lyes on the grass." '

In poetry such as this, so informed by the very spirit of its
subject, so free from the intrusion of any subjective and personal
element, in poetry such as this is offered a welcome relief from
the intensive individualism of modern verse. While progress
gives, even in the sphere of art, it is certain that progress also
takes away. If in the poetry of culture we meet many and
delightful qualities, it is no less true that in the poetry of primitive
periods, of periods ignorant of the principles by which we
suppose art to be governed, there are to be found other and
no less delightful qualities. The artist of the civilized community seems to have lost the art of arts, that of losing himself
in the intensity of his imaginative grasp of the subject, so that
his reader is left face to face with that alone. The names of
the makers of the ballads are forgotten, but their monuments
remain immortal, and, *pace* Sir Thomas Browne, who pitied
the founder of the Pyramids because his name had perished,
to leave a living work of art is far less a fruitful continuation
than to remain in the memory of the race crowned as king of
some barren territory. It is with these ballads as with Homer,
it matters little in the alembic of whose brain their phrases were
distilled.

' As one that for a weary space has lain
　　Lulled by the song of Circe and her wine
　　In gardens near the pale of Proserpine,
Where that Ægæan isle forgets the main,
And only the low lutes of love complain,
　　And only shadows of wan lovers pine,
　　As such an one were glad to know the brine
Salt on his lips, and the large air again,
So gladly, from the songs of modern speech
　　Men turn, and see the stars, and feel the free
　　Shrill wind beyond the close of heavy flowers
　　And through the music of the languid hours,
They hear like ocean on a western beach
　　The surge and thunder of the Odyssey.' [1]

To the students of folk-lore the European ballads offer a field from which a rich harvest may be reaped. The library collected by Child during the time that he was occupied upon his work amounted to about 7,000 volumes ; but it is not necessary to enter upon so exhaustive an enquiry as this fact suggests to glean much of interest from the study of ballad literature. To the students of mediæval superstitions, for example, these English and Scottish ballads offer a wealth of detail. Here are tales in which elves, water-nymphs, fairies, giants, dwarfs, mermen and maids, trolls and nixies, are plentiful ; here are spells and counter-spells, enchantments and disenchantments, transformations of human beings into beasts of the field, into fish and into trees. Here is a world in which the blood of children or of virgins will cure leprosy, in which disenchantment may be procured by a draught of blood or by a bath of milk, a world in which there are sure tests of fidelity in love : the unfaithful wife or husband may be detected by the use of a chair that cannot be sat in, a cup that cannot be drunk from by the faithless one, a ring which changes colour and betrays the guilty, a robe which refuses to be donned by

[1] Sonnet by Andrew Lang, prefixed to the translation of the ' Odyssey,' by Butcher and Lang.

the impure. This is the world, too, of omens and of riddles. In it one reads significance from the loss of a button or the heel of a shoe at the beginning of a journey; if one's horse stumbles or one's nose bleeds, the omen spells disaster. To dream of blood is an evil thing, and of ravens foretells the death of a near and dear friend. Only in this world may fair wives be won by guessing hard riddles set by cunning parents, or by asking one to which they fail to give an answer. To this world the dead return, and their kiss is fatal; they offer advice or administer punishment, and not seldom bear away with them to their own country the living, breathing mortal. But while it is a world of high and dread romance, it is also a world of uncompromising, full-blooded reality, of throbbing human life and feeling, of actual doing and suffering. Nor is it destitute of the salt of humour. Here is a passage from a spirited ballad describing the escape of Kinmont Willie across the Border from the hands of the English Governor of Carlisle:

> 'Buccleuch has turn'd to Eden water,
>   Even where it flowed frae bank to brim,
> And he has plung'd in wi' a' his band,
>   And safely swam them thro' the stream.
>
> 'He turn'd him on the other side,
>   And at Lord Scroope his glove flung he,
> "If ye like na my visit in merry England,
>   In fair Scotland come visit me."
>
> 'All sore astonished stood Lord Scroppe,
>   He stood as still as rock of stane;
> He scarcely dared to trew his eyes,
>   When thro' the water they had gane;
>
> '"He is either himsell a devil frae hell,
>   Or else his mother a witch maun be;
> I wad na have ridden that wan water,
>   For a' the gowd in Christentie."'

'Poetry, were it the rudest,' says Carlyle, 'so it be sincere, is the attempt which man makes to render his existence harmonious, the utmost he can do for that end ; it springs therefore from his whole feelings, opinions, activity, and takes its character from these. It may be called the music of his whole manner of being, and, historically considered, is the test how far Music or Freedom existed therein.'

The Romantic Revival

The terms *classic* and *romantic*, freely bandied about in the literary criticism of the last hundred years, can hardly be said to have attained any definite connotation, any sharp precision of meaning. The classic authors, *par excellence*, are the ancients, the makers of the literatures of Greece and Rome ; and the classics of our own or any other literature are the writers who best represent it, who have given to it whatever of beauty or of dignity it may possess. Thus far we speak the language of the market-place, and are intelligible to the average citizen ; but if we adopt the phrases of the schools, if we speak of the classics of our own literature as romantic in temper ; of some of the ancients, like Virgil, as no less so ; if we speak of classic subjects as treated by Marlowe or Shelley in the romantic manner, or of romantic subjects by Keats and Byron in the classic couplet, we introduce conceptions to the comprehension of which a course of literary history is the only avenue. It is, indeed, neither possible nor desirable to harden into absolute definition the general sense suggested by these terms, but because, however loosely they may be applied, they represent certain real characteristics, represent each a clearly marked group or blend of qualities, we are called upon to retain them, and to render to ourselves some account of them. The term *classic* needs no interpretation as regards origin—that which belongs to the first class—but a serviceable suggestion may be gleaned from the origin of the term *romantic*. When the northern barbarians streamed through the various gates of the declining Roman empire, and, victorious, imposed their rule upon the conquered Romans, they rendered a homage to the power that once had ruled the world by acknowledging the language of the conquered inhabitants as the language which best represented the results of civilization, as the language proper to the church, the school, and the law, the *lingua Latina*. But beside the purer language of the scholar, they found flourishing a language of the people, *lingua Romana rustica*, and with this the language of the conquering tribes was eventually mingled. The mother Latin thus became the parent of several daughters, the Romance languages. By *Romance* of course we mean no longer a language, but a type of composition, of which the poems and tales of the troubadours were the earliest specimens ; and as the new conditions of life gave birth to a literature which differed not merely in form, but in spirit and tone from the older literature, we come into possession of a term which is descriptive of that spirit and tone. Thus from the moment at which Renaissance influences are first apparent in our own literature, the need arises to distinguish by the terms *classic* and *romantic* the two clearly defined tendencies in art, the two clearly marked lines of artistic purpose discernible in the work of English writers. It may be said of Chaucer that he was at school in France and at the university in Italy ; his early poetical education was obtained in the school of the Romance writers, his later in the school of the Classical Revival. But the impulse generated by the Renaissance in the direction of a study and imitation of the classic literatures, though it assisted in the technical education of the English poets of the age of Elizabeth, did not, as in France, exert an immediate and overpowering influence upon our literature. In the Elizabethan drama, as represented by Marlowe and by Shakespeare, the romantic temper predominates, the romantic spirit is triumphant.

' Was this the face that launched a thousand ships,
    And burnt the topless towers of Ilium ?
    Sweet Helen, make me immortal with a kiss ! '

' I dreamt there was an emperor Antony ;—
    O, such another sleep, that I might see
    But such another man ! . . .
    His legs bestrid the ocean ; his reared arm

Crested the world : his voice was propertied
As all the tuned spheres, . . . in his livery
Walked crowns and crownets ; realms and islands were
As plates dropped from his pocket.'

Such passages vibrate to the true romantic string, but while the spirit of romance predominates in Elizabethan literature, while the romantic note rings clear above all others in it, a tendency may be read there, which was destined to outlast the romantic, was destined to a later, but no less complete a triumph. While Marlowe, and Spenser, and Shakespeare pursued the path along which they were guided by their own genius and the stronger impulses of the time, Ben Jonson, who was student and scholar no less than poet, pondering over the precedents and principles of art as exhibited in the works of ancient literature, endeavoured to frame for himself an *apparatus criticus* of precept and example, and as early as Spenser's university days a group of scholars and critics were ready to agree with Ascham that ' our rude beggarly rhyming was first brought into Italy by Goths and Huns, when all good verses and all good learning were destroyed by them.'

In France the Renaissance ideals achieved an immediate triumph, and from the foundation of the Academy in 1635, those ideals were enthroned in absolute authority, and the reign of the classical tradition assured. The English authors of the Elizabethan period remained for the most part un-trammelled by the classic tradition, about which they knew or cared little, and Jonson and Milton, who may be regarded as in one sense the last of the Elizabethans, were the first great English writers who followed by deliberate choice the traditions of classical rather than of English literature. Thus gradually was it, and not until the appeal made upon the imagination by the widening horizons of the physical and intellectual worlds began to prove less potent and stimulating, that the influence of the new learning makes itself fully felt, and the studies of the scholars shape the ideals of the republic of letters. What, then, were the qualities which the Renaissance found so admirable in the works of the ancients, what potent charm resided in those qualities strong enough to create an enthusiasm for the classic literatures which ripened later into something like a superstitious regard for them as divinely perfect, as literatures beside which those of the Romance languages were merely barbarous or Gothic?

All art springs from the instinctive human worship of the ideal, of perfection: art celebrates beauty, and ministers to the human desire for it. But to some races, as to some individuals, certain aspects of beauty make the most persuasive appeal, and to others certain other aspects. For one man the highest note in poetry is struck by such a passage as this from Wordsworth:

' The Form remains, the Function never dies;
  While we the brave, the mighty, and the wise,
  We men, who in our morn of youth defied
  The elements, must vanish:—be it so!
  Enough if something from our hands have power
  To live, and act, and serve the future hour:
  And if, as toward the silent tomb we go,
  Through love, through hope, and faith's transcendent dower,
  We feel that we are greater than we know.'

For another, the cup of intellectual delight brims over when magic accents such as these from Coleridge fall upon his ear:

' In Xanadu did Kubla Khan
  A stately pleasure-dome decree:
  Where Alph, the sacred river, ran
  Through caverns measureless to man,
        Down to a sunless sea.'

To the Greeks, the beauty which resides in form, in perfect proportions, made the most powerful appeal; hence in their sculpture, and in their architecture, the Greeks became the masters of the world. The classic spirit in art, too, is for ever associated with sharpness of intellectual outline, precision of design, with purity, and calm, and order. 'What is there lovely in poetry,' says Landor, 'unless there be moderation and composure?' The qualities which the Renaissance found admirable in ancient art were those which distinguished it from the romantic, the qualities of simplicity, repose, precision, order. These it found admirable because the mediæval world knew beauty under other and differing guises, and the noble simplicities of ancient art once known asserted a sovereign power. The aim of the classic artist—one may read it on every surviving work, on every magnificent fragment—was to elevate rather than to affect; the aim of the romantic artist to affect, and again affect, and once again affect. Thus classic art is dominated by the conception that only what is fully grasped, completely realized and understood, is suitable for artistic treatment; mediæval art is eager to suggest a significance, a depth of meaning, such as may, with however vague imaginings, dilate the soul.

Christian revelation, with its introduction of truths beyond precise comprehension, carried the artist of the Middle Ages into dealing with human life as an island in an ocean of mystery, but an ocean across which the light of heaven shone, across which the saints of God continually were privileged to journey. While, then, the classic spirit in art is associated with form, and calm, and order, the mediæval is suffused with colour, enthusiasm, and mystery; for the one believed in the senses and fed them with beauty, keeping as its ideal, 'self-reverence, self-knowledge, self-control,' the other discredited the earthly senses, and had for its ideal self-abandonment, a knowledge of God, and spiritual raptures. Approaching truth by analysis, Greek art draws in outline and speaks a direct language; approaching truth by intuition and faith, Christian art paints in colour and speaks in symbol. The Greek, like Sophocles, believed in the real world with all its certainties. He saw all that he did see with unfailing clearness of vision, and the spirit of precision and simplicity bears rule in the sphere of his artistic creation. The Christian of the middle ages, like Dante, believed in an invisible world, with all its terrors and splendours seen only by the eye of the soul ; and enthusiasm, inspired fervour, emotional glow, and a sense of reverence and of awe are the marks of his art.

In their reproduction of life in art the ancients, then, aimed at clearness and sharpness of outline, both in idea and language, and were thus content to win acceptance, not so much through the excitement resident in the subject as through their treatment of it.

> 'The charm of what is classical in art or literature,' wrote Walter Pater, 'is that of the well-known tale, to which we can nevertheless listen over and over again, because it is told so well. . . . It is the addition of strangeness to beauty that constitutes the romantic character in art. . . . It is the addition of curiosity to the desire for beauty that constitutes the romantic temper.'

'The essence of romance is mystery,' says another critic ; 'it is the sense of something hidden, of imperfect revelation.' The romantic artist, not content with the sharp, clear outline of the classical artist, desires to suggest, to arouse the feeling of expectation or of awe, of something yet untold. 'Clear, unimpassioned presentation of the subject, whether done in prose or verse, is the prominent feature of the classical style.' We may speak of the classical artist as disinterested : he stands aloof from his creations, they betray no trace of his personal affections, dislikes, enthusiasms. 'Homer,' says Landor, 'is subject to none of the passions, but he sends them all forth on their errands with as much precision as Apollo his golden arrows.'

While, then, ancient or classic art takes the world as it finds it, and imports into it no personal element, and few moral and intellectual problems, the romantic artist declines to accept the present and visible as the only sphere for art; and seeking in his own mind for sentiments and ideas, presents a new world, composed of the world as it appears to sense together with another, the world as it *might* be, or *will* be, or *ought* to be, or perhaps, if all were known, really *is*, a world drawn from his ideals, and feelings, and desires. Romanticism rejoices in the freshness and the glory of the exhaustless vistas and changing emotional and spiritual perspectives of the world; classicism in the sharply defined presentations of the intellect, the victory of reason over emotion as well as over the baffling problems of the soul. 'All art,' said Pater, 'constantly aspires towards the conditions of music'; and again it has been contended that the very perfection of lyrical poetry, which is artistically the highest and most complete form of poetry, seems to depend on 'a certain suppression or vagueness of mere subject.' These are *dicta* from the notebook of the romantic critic. He speaks of *mere subject*; with him the perfection of poetry is reached when meaning is almost lost in an excess of sensuous suggestiveness. He desires to affect. With Aristotle the lyric was not the highest and most complete form of poetry, and architectonics, constructive power, design, ranked far above the mere accessories of music and diction. He desires to elevate. If bred in the classical school, the critic's first requirement in poetry is that it should be articulate, else how can it serve the reason? Matthew Arnold's preference was consequently enlisted on the side of the poetry which made for intellectual clearness and moral force, for the poetry which touched life at the greatest number of points of human interest, and illuminated or interpreted it. The most artistic poetry for Arnold was poetry such as this:

'If thou didst ever hold me in thy heart,
    Absent thee from felicity awhile,
And in this harsh world draw thy breath in pain
    To tell my story.'

With Pater it would have been poetry such as this, which weaves a fantasy around the song of the nightingale :

> ' The voice I hear this passing night was heard
>   In ancient days by emperor and clown ;
> Perhaps the selfsame song that found a path
>   Through the sad heart of Ruth, when, sick for home,
> She stood in tears amid the alien corn ;
>   The same that ofttimes hath
> Charmed magic casements, opening on the foam
>   Of perilous seas, in faery lands forlorn.'

When one is asked to make choice between passages such as these, exhibiting poetry at its best in different moods, one is reminded of the children's game in which the delicate question is secretly proposed to each player in turn, ' Would you rather have a golden apple or a golden pear ? ' and the answer enlists him in one or other of two opposing camps. Some of us insist on the qualities of the golden apple, on truth and high seriousness, on intellectual and moral insight in poetry ; some on the qualities of the golden pear, on sensuous and emotion-stirring powers, on perfume and bouquet, on music and mystery. There exists no need at this time to rank the apple before the pear, or to disparage its qualities beside those of its more luscious companion. But we must note that from the moment at which the fountains of the Elizabethan inspiration began to fail, and writers, with a student's enthusiasm, to seek for principles to guide their efforts, the qualities of ancient poetry attracted a continually deepening and widening appreciation. Yet because the genius of Greek literature declined to yield up the secret of its subtle perfections to an age in which scholarship was young,[1] the English writers of the Augustan age failed to reproduce anything of the Greek spirit in their work, and

[1] Bentley's comment upon Pope's *Homer*—' A very pretty poem, Mr. Pope, but you must not call it Homer '—may perhaps stand as the first record in English of a true appreciation of the distinctive genius of Greek poetry.

were successful only in reproducing something of the spirit of Latin literature, a literature imitative and disciplined, majestic but measured, regular, orderly, formal, sober in subject and manner. Propriety of language, correctness and precision, restraint and moderation, these words express the lessons learned from the Roman authors by Dryden and his successors. And in the sphere of prose the lessons were of inestimable value. The gain to English poetry is not so obvious. However willing we may be to retain for the school of Pope and Johnson the title of the classical school of English poetry, it is evident that the writers who belonged to it neither appreciated profoundly the true character of Hellenic and Roman art, nor did they succeed in imitating it with the closeness desired. Dryden and Pope and Johnson exhibit the qualities of simplicity, repose, precision, and these have been named as classic qualities, But they attain them by limiting the scope of their undertakings. They are simple because they deal only with the familiar facts of life ; calm, because they have never known what it is to be profoundly moved ; precise, because they merely repeat in terser phrase the current opinions of the time. Simplicity, repose, precision are only admirable and precious, are only *classic*, when threatened by imaginative wealth, emotional fervour, intellectual profundity. But the poets of the Augustan age were in perfect security from these splendid dangers. Pope, as Johnson said, ' wrote in such a manner as might expose him to few hazards.' The times, indeed, were not in need of poetry ; prose satisfied the pressing intellectual needs of the majority. How little was the necessity felt for poetry at all is seen in the words of Pope : ' I chose verse because I could express ideas more shortly than in prose itself.' Pope chose verse not because he felt the need of verse, but because he found it a superior kind of prose. It might not be too much to say that with the majority of any period prose answers every need of their natures. But with the middle of the eighteenth century came a demand for something more than a superior prose, and we may think accurately of the Romantic Revival as a reaction in favour of poetry as against prose. The qualities which the writers of the Augustan Age lacked, even in their poetry, were precisely the qualities which make poetry, which go to distinguish it from prose, and the Romantic Revival was the outcome of a need for a medium of fuller expression felt by the spiritual and emotional part of human nature, which had for a time suffered eclipse. The character of English literature in the eighteenth century may be summed up by saying that its appeal was an appeal almost exclusively to the intelligence ; it looked upon man as if he were of intelligence all compact, and was not ruled by feeling and instinct and intuition and fancy in a greater degree than by the lucubrations of his reason. The Romantic Revival enthroned in the room of reason and of law, aspirations, desires, ideals—in a word, absolute though unattainable perfection in the place of relative perfection, represented by tolerable social and political institutions. With the Revolution at the end of the century came the idea of

> ' the ultimate angels' law,
> Indulging every instinct of the soul,
> There where law, life, joy, impulse are one thing.'

It may be paradoxical to assert that the interests of the Augustan Age were not literary or artistic, that they were political or religious ; but the literature of the period is a series of practical and polemical pamphlets, prose and verse, into which are compressed the best ideas, the most cogent arguments connected with questions of the day. ' Subjects of importance to society ' were the poet's themes, what interested ' the Town ' his business. Hence is it that the age of Anne adored in literature the neat, the finished, the complete, in a word the finite, and the men of letters chose to treat in art only such subjects as lent themselves to a presentation in sharp, clear outlines, topics in which no mystery lurked, and upon which expressions of final opinion were possible. Thus was the sphere of art cabin'd and confined, and no room could be found for lyric poetry in a generation whose interests were practical, and could not therefore be sung about.

It is not surprising that such an age should dislike obscurity and extravagance, enthusiasm or intemperate emotion, and should correspondingly admire clearness, precision, moderation, and common sense ; that it should ridicule the ' metaphysical ' poets who had carried the Elizabethan characteristics to excess ; that it should hold as barbarous and Gothic Spenser and Marlowe, and prefer Chaucer in a version by Dryden ; that it should lack interest in nature, and find in the social life of the town the only pleasures worthy of the cultivated man.

It will not do to think of the Romantic Revival as a protest against classical qualities in poetry, or as arising out of a mere desire for the new and strange ; it had its origin in a gradual recognition of the inadequate account virtually taken of human nature by the current mode of thought in the early eighteenth century. Even during the undisputed sovereignty of the Augustan tradition, an individual author here and there showed in his writings that he harboured treasonable ideas. A writer like Allan Ramsay not only harboured treasonable ideas, but indulged in treasonable practices. As Shairp says, ' Ramsay had the courage, in a conventional time both in English and Scottish poetry, to recognize and be true to the manners, the simple everyday life, the rural character, and the scenery of his native land.' Others, like Parnell and William Hamilton, the author of the *Braes of Yarrow*, might be cited as secret traitors, the pioneers of revolution. We can conceive the more imaginative minds of the time protesting that the world of moderation and good taste and common sense was a somewhat dull world, in which there was little to interest and less to attract or charm ; we can conceive the growth of an appetite for something more emotional in poetry or more stimulating in philosophy. The tide of opinion gradually rose until it became possible for heresy to appear in print unabashed, such heresy as Joseph Warton's, for example, who wrote in 1756 :

> ' I revere the memory of Pope, I respect and honour his abilities, but I do not think him at the head of his profession. In other words, in that species of poetry wherein Pope excelled, he is superior to all mankind, and I only say that this species of poetry is not the most excellent one of the art.'

That in the representative poetry of the time certain qualities essential to poetry were absent, that in the representative philosophy of the time only a small part of the actual truth about things was told, could only be convictions of gradual growth. In the real world, in the world there could be no mistake about, the eighteenth century had a profound belief. But common-sense realism turns its back upon truth by declining to investigate it. And in effect we can imagine the early Romanticists asking the exasperating question, What is the real world ? In the account given of the universe by some enthusiastic scientists a generation ago, the eighteenth-century point of view recurred, and when the metaphysician inquired innocently enough, What is the real world ? he acted again the part unconsciously played in the domain of æsthetics by the revolutionaries. The world of eighteenth-century art and philosophy was the world so far as it was thoroughly understood. But the world as far as it is fully understood falls far short of the real world, said the Romanticists. The sphere of art is not the apparent world of reality : to art belongs the right and privilege of entrance into the larger reality, it emancipates man from the bondage of his little circumscribed life of conventions and customs and routine, and makes him a citizen of the universe. And so when Pater says, ' It is the addition of strangeness to beauty that constitutes the romantic character in art,' he is expressing only a half-truth, for a large part of the delight which the poetry of Romanticism can give arises out of a recognition that the poet has penetrated to a higher sphere of reality than that in which we are accustomed to move, and we appreciate not the strangeness but the truth of his conception. Take the nature poetry of Wordsworth—take a poem like that entitled *The Education of Nature* :

'Three years she grew in sun and shower,
  Then Nature said, "A lovelier flower
On earth was never sown ;
  This Child I to myself will take ;
She shall be mine, and I will make
  A Lady of my own.

.   .   .   .   .

'"She shall be sportive as the fawn
  That wild with glee across the lawn
Or up the mountain springs ;
  And hers shall be the breathing balm,
And hers the silence and the calm
  Of mute insensate things.

'"The floating clouds their state shall lend
  To her ; for her the willow bend ;
Nor shall she fail to see
  Even in the motions of the Storm
Grace that shall mould the Maiden's form
  By silent sympathy.

'"The stars of midnight shall be dear
  To her ; and she shall lean her ear
In many a secret place
  Where rivulets dance their wayward round,
And beauty born of murmuring sound
  Shall pass into her face."'

Is this a string of conceits, or is it a profound philosophy ? If your feelings respond to verses such as these, you are a true child of the Romantic Revival, or rather you are a human being with needs other than mere intellectual needs, a human being open to impressions from 'worlds unrealized,' and possessed of sympathies which admit you into the secret councils of the universal mind. But it cannot be too frequently emphasized that the Romantic Revival was not a revolt against the methods of ancient classic art ; a revolt rather against the poetry which addressed itself exclusively to the intelligence, and which had arisen out of an appreciation of certain qualities of Latin poetry that were readily apparent in it and characteristic of its peculiar genius. It was a protest raised by the imagination and the emotions. And that protest was first made in the reaction against the heroic couplet, a form specially adapted for the poetry of syllogism and epigram, of satire and dissertation, and almost exclusively employed in the unemotional and unimaginative verse of the time.

All through the eighteenth century was waged the literary controversy between the defenders of the heroic couplet against blank verse and the unconscious forerunners of the Romantic school who attacked it. The value of rhyme was found by Dryden to be, that 'it bounds and circumscribes the fancy. For imagination in a poet is a faculty so wild and lawless, that, like a high-ranging spaniel, it must have clogs tied to it, lest it outrun the judgment. The great easiness of blank verse renders the poet too luxuriant.' [1] Or in other words, moderation, restraint, regularity, order, what is there in poetry which can compensate for the absence of these ? The first poem of any importance after Milton, written in blank verse, was Thomson's *Seasons* in 1726, the next was Young's *Night Thoughts* in 1742. From this time blank verse grew in favour with the more imaginative writers, and with its revival came the revival of the sonnet and some of the earlier English lyrical measures. But the reappearance of the Spenserian stanza as a popular form is a more important indication of the change in taste than any other, and for this reason, that Spenser was looked upon by the orthodox in matters literary during the eighteenth

[1] Dedicatory Epistle to *The Rival Ladies*, 1664.

century as *par excellence* the representative of the extravagant and wild, of the Gothic in poetry, an epitome of the qualities to be repudiated by the lovers of true excellence. When moved to praise Spenser or Shakespeare, the critic had to vindicate his possession of good taste by reservations, as did Addison :

> ' Old Spenser next, warmed with poetic rage,
> *In ancient tales amused a barbarous age* ;
> An age that yet uncultivate and rude,
> Where'er the poet's fancy led, pursued
> Through pathless fields, and unfrequented floods,
> To dens of dragons and enchanted woods.
> But now the mystic tale that pleased of yore
> *Can charm an understanding age no more.*'

What illumination there is in the complacent phrase, ' an understanding age ' ! Addison's diagnosis of the character of his times was excellent, but his range of vision did not permit him to foresee that the protest of the future would be raised against the limitations his words unconsciously announce. Time has imported a similar irony into the remark of John Hughes, an early eighteenth-century editor of Spenser—' To compare the *Faerie Queene* with the models of antiquity would be like drawing a parallel between the Roman and the Gothic architecture.'

A number of Spenserian imitations nevertheless appeared in the eighteenth century, and from 1725 to 1750 the Spenserian heresy made considerable progress. Thomson, by his *Castle of Indolence* (1748), increased his claim to attention as a fore-runner of the revolution, more especially as he exhibited traces of true romantic feeling, and was not merely engaged, as were the majority of the revivers of the earlier verse forms, in pouring the old wine of conventional sentiment into the new bottles of resuscitated metres. In 1757 Dr. Johnson, the guardian of the sacred Augustan tradition, became alarmed. The imitators

H

of Spenser waxed numerous, heresy was rampant, and the champion of orthodoxy strode into the arena. In the *Rambler* of May 14, 1757, he wrote : ' The imitation of Spenser by the influence of some men of learning and genius seems likely to gain upon the age.'—' His style was in his own time allowed to be vicious. . . . His stanza is at once difficult and unpleasing ; tiresome to the ear by its monotony, and to the attention by its length.'—' The style of Spenser might by long labour be justly copied ; but life is surely given us for higher purposes than to gather what our ancestors have thrown away, and to learn what is of no value, but because it has been forgotten.'

One can barely imagine a literary conservatism more complete than that of Johnson ; with Pope the end of the world had come, all things were consummated.

' By perusing the works of Dryden, Pope discovered the most perfect fabric of English verse, and habituated himself to that only which he found the best ; in consequence of which restraint his poetry has been censured as too uniformly musical, and as glutting the ear with unvaried sweetness. . . . New sentiments and new images others may produce ; but to attempt any further improvement in versification will be dangerous. Art and diligence have now done their best, and what shall be added will be the effort of tedious toil and needless curiosity.'

The imitations of Spenser herald the approaching change in literary fashion, but it is noteworthy that the poets who did the best service in the cause of Romanticism were rather students in the school of Milton than of Spenser, a proof that it was not against classic qualities but against the poetry of mere intelligence that the revolt was directed. Milton was a better scholar than either Pope or Dryden, he modelled his great epics upon the works of the ancient poets : his *Samson Agonistes* is the best example of a drama in the Attic manner that English literature possesses, his *Lycidas* is suffused with memories of the

Greek ; but for all this the spirit of his poetry was felt to be more romantic than classic, as the eighteenth century understood those terms. But Milton's scholarship enabled him to assimilate the true spirit of the ancients, to learn of them something more than their negative virtues of restraint and discipline and precision, and while preserving these virtues to give at the same time free scope to his imagination. Though he lacks the passion and emotion which the later school of Romance desired, there is no English poetry which more powerfully dilates the imagination ; and to his earlier poems Collins and Gray were indebted for the impulse which gave them their place as leaders in the early stages of the revolutionary movement. The ' longing for a shudder,' which is present in the poetry of the Romantic Revival, presents in an exaggerated form the revolt against the tyranny of convention. But it must not be named as its sole constituent. A poem of Warton's, published in 1740, entitled *The Enthusiast ; or the Lover of Nature,* presents another aspect of the new tendency : the fancy for wildness or solitude in landscape, for woods and mountains, ruined castles and twilight groves, such scenes, in short, as might feed the emotions, and stimulate the imagination. ' It may certainly,' as Courthope says, ' be regarded as the starting-point of the Romantic Revival, as it expresses all that love of solitude and that yearning for the spirit of a bygone age which are especially associated with the genius of the Romantic school of poetry.' Another volume of poems, published in 1746 by Joseph Warton, is avowedly romantic in character. In the preface the author remarks that he looks upon ' invention and imagination to be the chief faculties of a poet, so he will be happy if the following odes may be looked upon as an attempt to bring back poetry into its right channel.' The early poetry of Romanticism, both that of the brothers Warton and their contemporaries, is characterized by a strain of melancholy : a vein of sombre reflection runs through it. Elegies were for a time a favourite form of composition, and ' graveyard poetry '

was not a little appreciated.[1]   The following from Warton are
characteristic verses :

> 'Haste Fancy from the scenes of folly
> To meet the matron Melancholy,
> Goddess of the tearful eye,
> That loves to fold her arms and sigh ;
> *Let us with silent footsteps go*
> *To charnels and the house of woe,*
> *To Gothic churches, vaults and tombs*
> Where each sad night a virgin comes
> With throbbing breast and faded cheek
> Her promised bridegroom's urn to seek.'

But ' the whole Romantic school,' as Lowell wrote, ' in its
germ no doubt, but unmistakably foreshadowed, lies already
in the *Ode on the Superstitions of the Highlands*.' This poem,
written by Collins about 1750, was not published until 1788,
perhaps because it was not thought suited to the spirit of the
times, but exhibits even in its title the new literary attitude
—' An Ode on the Popular Superstitions of the Highlands of
Scotland ; *considered as the subject of poetry*.' In praising the
Highland superstitions as good subjects for poetry, Collins thus
addresses Home, the author of *Douglas* :

> 'Fresh to that soil thou turn'st, where every vale
> Shall prompt the poet, and his song demand ;
> To thee thy copious subjects ne'er shall fail ;
> Thou needst but take thy pencil in thy hand,
> And paint what all believe, who own thy genial land.'

Here is the kernel of the whole matter, the conviction that
outside the world of reality and common sense, as represented
in polite society and the opinions of cultivated men, as limited
by the current philosophy, were to be found subjects adapted
for poetic treatment.   About the time that Collins was engaged
upon this poem, Gray completed his famous *Elegy*. In his

---

[1] *E.g.* Parnell's *Night-Piece on Death*, and Blair's *Grave*, 1743.

earliest poems, he betrays no trace of romantic predilections, the *Elegy* marks an indeterminate period ; but in *The Progress of Poesy*, 1754, and *The Bard*, 1757, we see him well on his way towards the camp of the liberals, and in *The Descent of Odin*, 1761, enrolled as a recruit in the rapidly swelling forces of the revolution. How is one to explain Gray's conversion ? It may be ascribed without hesitation to the critical movement, which accompanied and supported the new poetic impulse. In 1755 Professor Mallet of Copenhagen published an *Introduction to the History of Denmark*, and in the following year added a volume upon the mythology and poetry of the Celts, and particularly of the ancient Scandinavians. This book marks the awakening of the modern historic sense, the birth of European interest in ancient and mediæval history, and at once exercised a potent influence upon the thought of the day. Gray was profoundly impressed, and when in 1760 *Fragments of Ancient Poetry collected in the Highlands of Scotland and translated from the Gaelic or Erse Language* [1] appeared, his adhesion to the cause of Romanticism was sealed. Public taste was ripe for the reception of the work of the antiquarian and poet, and when in 1765 Percy published his famous *Reliques of Ancient Poetry* (preceded by *Five Pieces of Runic Poetry* in 1763), and in 1770 his translation of Mallet's books, the popular imagination was at once captivated, and the stream was soon running strongly in favour of the Gothic barbarians. In this suddenly awakened interest in the past we have of course one of the chief characteristics of the Romantic movement. The intellectual horizon was immeasurably extended, and as in the Elizabethan age the strange tales brought back by the adventurers of the new world beyond the seas at once aroused and delighted the imagination, so these stories and ballads of a past and forgotten age, the marvels of the northern mythologies recovered by the students of antiquity, stimulated and delighted the more imaginative

[1] The work of Macpherson, who followed it up in 1762 and 1763 by translations of *Ossian*.

minds of the eighteenth century, weary of conventional good taste and common sense. In order to appreciate the electric thrill with which, despite the passionate scorn of Dr. Johnson, Macpherson's *Ossian* was received, it is only necessary to read, after a few lines of polite eighteenth-century poetry by Pope or some members of his school, a few lines of its vague and sugges-tive declamations :

'I have seen the walls of Balclutha, but they were desolate. The fire had resounded in the halls, and the voice of the people is heard no more. The stream of Clutha was removed from its place by the fall of the walls. The thistle shook there its lonely head ; the moss whistled to the wind. The fox looked out of the windows ; the rank grass of the wall waved round its head. Desolate is the dwelling of Moina ; silence is in the house of her fathers. Raise the song of mourning, O bards ! over the land of strangers.'

After Pope's most admired epigrams,

' 'Tis from high life high characters are drawn :
A saint in crape is twice a saint in lawn,'

how enchanting, too, must have sounded the antique vigour of the ballad,

' The King sits in Dunfermline town,
Drinking the bluid-red wine ! '

Mallet's book on the Scandinavian mythology represents the positive side of the critical movement, while Joseph Warton's *Essay on Pope*, published the year following (1756), is repre-sentative of its negative side, denying, as it does, to the Augustan poetry the possession of the final virtues.

But the effects of the revolution in taste were not confined to poetry, or even to literature in general. If we turn to Gray's Letters and Journals we shall find sentences breathing new and surprising sentiments.—' In our little journey up to the Grande Chartreuse,' he writes to his friend West, ' I do not remember to have gone ten paces without an exclamation that there was no restraining. Not a precipice, not a torrent, not a cliff, but is *pregnant with religion and poetry*.' But if Gray was one of the earliest writers who discovered that mountains were to be admired, Horace Walpole, as has been frequently noted, was ' almost the first modern Englishman who found out that our cathedrals were really beautiful.' During the eighteenth century the classical style in architecture completely predominated. Early in the century the palaces of Blenheim and Castle Howard were erected in it, and the preference gradually led to its adoption for all classes of buildings, public or domestic. Like Percy, Walpole was an enthusiastic anti- quarian, and in 1747 made the first attempt in England to revive the Gothic style. The sham battlements of the famous ' Gothic castle,' Strawberry Hill, are a landmark in connection with the birth of modern historical and antiquarian interest. But in 1764 Walpole erected still another Gothic building in his novel *The Castle of Otranto*, which, although like its pre- decessor a sham structure, supplied to the novel some of the modern ingredients wanting in the fiction of Defoe. Defoe belonged to the age of prose : a journalist who was in the habit of reporting daily occurrences, and whose stories are merely such reports, differing from those of the newspaper only in this, that they are occurrences that had not occurred. In his narratives there is a marked absence of poetry and sentiment ; nor does Pope in his *Essay on Man* better display the spirit of the eighteenth century than Defoe in *Robinson Crusoe*. To the novel Walpole added the vein of heightened emotion desired by the time, and the element of mystery in character and situation. The host of his imitators proclaims the age hungry for sensation. In Miss Clara Reeve's *Old English Baron*, Beck- ford's *Vathek*, Mrs. Radcliffe's *Sicilian Romance* and *The Mys- teries of Udolpho*, and in Lewis's *Monk*, the interest is of an intense and agitating character, the scenery wild and suggestive, the characters strange, violent, supernatural. The school of fiction which grew immediately out of the Romantic Revival represents its features in an exaggerated form ; true and false Romanticism were not yet distinguished. The appetite was yet too strong to discriminate, or to discern in Strawberry Hill, *Ossian,* or *The Castle of Otranto,* the unreal and the counterfeit element.

At the head of another group of writers who assisted in the emancipation of the natural life of the feelings stands the author of *Pamela,* and *Clarissa Harlowe,* published in 1748. Richardson's ' Romances of the heart' heralded one aspect of the revolt against the supremacy of the intelligence, and not only vindicated the right of the emotions to legitimate expression, but assigned to them their natural place as guides to conduct and ministers to delight. With Richardson the word ' sentimental,' now fallen to baser uses, meant little more than the cultivation of the feelings. But with Sterne, sentimentalism begins to run to waste, and becomes a prevailing mood which regards emotion as an end in itself, nor cares to determine its appropriate occasions or objects. In Henry Mackenzie's *Man of Feeling,* published in 1771, we reach the limits of which this style is capable, we assist at the carnival of the sentiments, we learn that there is such a thing as luxury in grief. But while Sterne took advantage of the emotional necessities of the time to trick his readers into tears, a nobler use of its susceptibilities was made by Wesley. A frank supernaturalist, Wesley's triumph by an appeal rather to the emotions than to the reason affords an important clue to the social and moral needs of his generation. The Romantic movement, indeed, regarded in all its bearings, exhibits the development of the humanitarian out of the political ideal, a cause in which the notion of a return to nature, promulgated by Rousseau, who visited England in 1766, did so great a service. With that herald of the Revolution a return to nature was a return to a less elaborately organized, a simpler political system, where kings and priests could imprison neither the intellects nor the sentiments of men. But the theories of fraternity and equality which inflamed the enthusiasm of France made no impression upon the colder-spirited islanders. Abstract doctrines sown in English fields send up no terrible crop of armed men. Later in the century, William Blake, born in 1757, stood out boldly in the great cause of liberty and democratic ideals. But Blake as artist and poet represents a later stage in the development of English thought. From boyhood a dreamy mystic to whom visions of angels were familiar, his best artistic work recalls that of Dürer and the mediæval painters ; throughout life he believed himself to be guided by ministers from the spiritual world, and he accounts for the greater part of his literary work as communicated to him by the spirit of a dead brother. Blake's singular independence of prevailing fashion, literary and artistic, is hardly matched in the history of our literature. Both as artist and as poet he expresses the life of a later generation nourished on a more spiritual philosophy, a nobler political and social creed, a poetry emancipated from the influences of a mechanic age.

No historian of the Romantic Revival could overlook the part played by the writers, like Warton and Hurd, who contributed to the liberalization of criticism. Warton's *Observations on the Faerie Queene* (1753), and Hurd's *Letters on Chivalry and Romance*, display the conscious side of a movement which was in the main unconscious, or rather they display the effort made by the analytical minds to understand and explain to themselves what the majority were content to feel. Yet it was not from England that the ideals of a criticism which should form part of a universal philosophy first emanated : the shaping ideas of the future issued from Germany, and their history in this country belongs to the early years of the nineteenth century. Upon the later history of Romanticism in England, of its association with revolutionary and democratic ideals, I do not propose to enter ; that later history, is it not written large that all may read in the poetry of Shelley and of Scott, of Wordsworth and of Coleridge and of Keats, is it not the history of English literature and art in the nineteenth century?

The early Romanticists had a mission to fulfil, and they fulfilled it by saying in effect to the generation to which they belonged, in the words of Hamlet to Horatio, ' There are more things in heaven and earth than are dreamt of in your philosophy.' It sounded the first few notes of a music which later became orchestral—the music of passion and of triumph, of passion for humanity in its long upward struggle, and of the emancipated imagination which frames for humanity ever new ideals. It opened out of a conventional age a little wicket-gate into a world outside that of our own immediate and circumscribed experience, into a world that we cannot enter unless imagination and faith take us by the hand and make us free of its mysteries, its aspirations, its hopes, its sympathies, and its thoughts ' that do often lie too deep for tears.'

If we would sum up our impressions we may think of the Romantic Revival as the revolt of the natural man against the artificial, the revolt of the imagination and the feelings against the insolent domination of the intelligence in the literature of England from Dryden to Johnson. It displays itself at first by a renewed interest in the works of the older English writers, turning from French models to the imitation of their works, and adopting their metrical forms in the place of the heroic couplet almost exclusively employed by the Augustan poets. It displays itself later by a revival of taste for anything mediæval, for Gothic in preference to classical architecture, by its interest in ancient ballad poetry, fostered by Percy's *Reliques* and similar collections, by its interest in the early history, the sagas and picturesque mythology of the Scandinavian and of the Celtic races, fostered by various antiquarian works and by the poems of Ossian. It displays itself by a renewed feeling for external nature, more especially in the wilder and more rugged types of scenery which most stimulate the imagination and the emotions. It displays itself by the appearance of a school of critics, a school of poets, a school of Romance writers, a school of novelists, expressing unconsciously or avowedly these predilections.

It would be vain to attempt any classification of latter-day writers which should assign them places in opposing camps. The wizard stream of romance has flowed into the sacred stream of poetry. It is not the poetry that can be most unreservedly labelled Romantic that we find irresistible, but that poetry which is above classification, which, while it excludes nothing that touches humanity from its world of subjects, displays in its expression the exactness, the dignity, the composure, the restraint that we associate with Sophocles or Lucretius, while at its heart burns the passion and the fire of Dante or of Burns. That strain is sometimes heard in the work of the Romanticists, sometimes in the work of the writers we name classical ; for it is simply the strain of poetry at its highest reach, the poetry that never fails to tranquillize or satisfy, to whose appeal in any preoccupation we can never be blind or deaf. Here we may surrender ourselves to the influences that belong to the divine beauty that ever brings consolation if it brings sadness, and can fortify the heart in the presence of Tragedy.

Wordsworth

I

Wordsworth was the only English poet who cared to write for us the history of his mind. The poet's life indeed is usually devoid of the romantic and adventurous elements which so attract us to the biographies of men of action or of affairs. Its interest lies within the region of psychology, but the material for this psychology is rarely provided. In Wordsworth's case alone, since he anxiously observed the operations of his own mind, and the movements of his affections, is it singularly full and complete. And *The Prelude*, which tells the story, is thus unique among English poems, possessed of a double value—the value of an authentic philosophical document and the value of art.

Like the rest of the author's poetry, *The Prelude* is beyond all else trustworthy. We know when we read Wordsworth that we are reading a single-minded and utterly sincere poet, who never poses, who has little delight in phrase-making, who prefers, and always prefers, truth to pungency and piquancy of expression. To his entire trustworthiness we may add lucidity. Describing, as he often describes, complex and elusive aspects of his inner life, simplicity never fails him. None can mistake Wordsworth's meaning anywhere or at any time. To sincerity and lucidity we must again add an incomparable quality— originality. Wordsworth borrowed nothing of consequence, his poetry is the perfectly genuine product of the contact of his own mind with nature and the world.

Here, then, are three great things. The poetry of Wordsworth is sincere, we can trust it ; it is lucid, we can understand it ; it is original, there is nothing elsewhere like it in the world. It may fail at times in other qualities, but these are its abiding attributes ; to these it owes its unceasing and unchallengeable power. And in no single poem are they more admirably

blended than in *The Prelude*, where the poet speaks of himself
and is himself. It is the priceless and the only needed com-
mentary on the aims and attainments of his life.

In the early part of this book the author describes his return
to the country of the lakes and hills—his return, after the
wanderings of his youth, to the places he had known in childhood. Making his escape from the city, where he 'had
pined a discontented sojourner,' he shook off his 'unnatural
self,' and with it—

> 'The heavy weight of many a weary day
> Not mine and such as were not made for me,'

and as preparation for the great poetic task he had braced
himself to perform, that he might gain further strength and fix
the wavering balance of his mind, he endeavours to recall his
most impressionable years, and the influences which during
these years moulded his character and determined his career.
And it would seem that impersonal powers rather than individuals were his earliest teachers. Already at ten years of age
he 'held unconscious intercourse with beauty old as creation
itself,' and his

> 'Brain
> Worked with a dim and undetermined sense
> Of unknown modes of being.'

As in a dream he felt himself surrounded by mighty presences,
living powers and towering forms, in the sky above his head and
the mountains that stood around his home. They passed into
his life and memory, and 'daily the common round of visible
things grew dear' to him, until at length as the years passed on,

> 'From Nature and her overflowing soul
> I had received so much that all my thoughts
> Were steeped in feeling : I was only then
> Contented, when with bliss ineffable
> I felt the sentiment of Being spread
> O'er all that moves and all that seemeth still.'

To this early intercourse with nature—the hills, the lakes and cataracts, the stars and clouds, the mists and winds, companions of his youth, Wordsworth ascribed his enduring peace of mind, his indifference to the standards of the world, his more than Roman confidence in the native strength of man, the never-failing fountain of joy which renewed itself perpetually in his own heart. Yet he is careful to tell us that he retained his mental independence unimpaired, and

> 'That by the regular action of the world
> My soul was unsubdued.'

We are asked at times to believe, but we are debarred from believing, that Wordswoth was a nature-intoxicated man, sunk in the larger life of which he was thus early conscious.

> 'An auxiliary light
> Came from my mind, which on the setting sun
> Bestowed new splendours ; the melodious birds,
> The fluttering breezes, fountains that run on
> Murmuring so sweetly in themselves, obeyed
> A like dominion, and the midnight storm
> Grew darker in the presence of my eye.'

We should miss the essential elements in his character, we should fail to understand him or his poetry, if we thought of this poet as a gentle dreamy youth, easily impressed, played upon by the chance winds and currents of his time and station. He was not such a youth. His clay was of a stiff, unyielding texture ; he held his own way through life, and held it with tenacity. At Cambridge he shared in the ordinary routine of the University, not untouched indeed by memories of the past in that ' garden of great intellects,' yet hardly changed in spirit, uninspired and undisturbed by its activities and ideals. Nor as a reader was he more easily subdued, for at no season of his life was he overcome by authors or their books, but retained from first to last a certain indifference to all printed things which astonished and exercised his friends.

An interest in human nature appears first to have fully awakened in Wordsworth's mind during a vacation spent at Hawkshead. There he noted the simple lives of the country people, and tells us that

' Shepherds were the men that pleased me first.'

But man was still subordinate to nature, and still the most moving spectacle for him was some morning or evening splendour of the hills—

<blockquote>
' Magnificent
The morning rose, in memorable pomp,
Glorious as e'er I had beheld—in front
The sea lay laughing at a distance ; near
The solid mountains shone, bright as the clouds,
Grain-tinctured, drenched in empyrean light.
And in the meadows and the lower grounds
Was all the sweetness of a common dawn—
Dews, vapours, and the melody of birds,
And labourers going forth to till the fields.'
</blockquote>

Wordsworth left Cambridge in 1789, and in 1789 all eyes were turned towards France. The following year he landed at Calais on ' the very eve of that great Federal day,' July 14, the day on which the King swore allegiance to the new constitution, the day on which the trees of liberty were planted all over the country. ' We crossed,' he said, ' at a time when the whole nation was mad with joy '—

<blockquote>
' France standing on the top of golden hours
And human nature seeming born again.'
</blockquote>

Wordsworth was a convinced friend of Revolutionary doctrine and was himself prepared to take an active share in the work that lay before the leaders of the people, nor did the Reign of

Terror shake his convictions. He believed that if liberty had to be purchased at a price, the price must be paid.

> 'Not caring if the wind did now and then
> Blow keen upon an eminence that gave
> Prospect so large into futurity.'

Even when England joined the enemies of France he was disappointed, not discouraged ; for, though a friend of his native land, he was before all a friend of freedom. But when with the advent of Napoleon the sword of defence was returned to its scabbard and that of conquest unsheathed, when France marched to the wars of national aggrandizement, Wordsworth faltered. He was compelled to a deeper stratum of reflection. It was natural that a young poet, led by generous instincts along a path which raised no doubts, suggested no problems, who had joyfully enlisted without shadow of hesitation in the grand old cause of liberty and humanity, should now find himself in the grasp of a great dilemma. It was natural that he should turn from the sphere of instinct and feeling, and apply to reason for assistance. It was the turn of reason now to hold aloft the torch and show her guiding light. But reason failed Wordsworth in his hour of need. Perplexed and distressed, he found no clue to the labyrinth of social and moral problems into which he was suddenly plunged. In the debate within his mind, argument was met by counter-argument, impulse checked by judgment, and motives dissected,

> 'Till, demanding formal proof,
> And seeking it in everything, I lost
> All feeling of conviction, and in fine,
> Sick, wearied out with contrarieties,
> Yielded up moral questions in despair.'

Wordsworth's faith in human nature had been shaken, and with it his faith in reason. And in this analytic mood, when he turned back to his old companion Nature for support and consolation, he found here too that it was possible to

> ' Unsoul
> As readily by syllogistic words
> Those mysteries of being which have made,
> And shall continue evermore to make,
> Of the whole human race one brotherhood.'

By the application of the analytic method the sun was driven from heaven, the light died out on the hills and meadows, the healing influences withdrew themselves, and the visible universe became a mere congregation of atoms gathered and dispelled in the blind battle of contending forces. He found, as was said of Pomponatius, ' what all men who think long enough and deep enough will find—that the action of pure intellect in relation to vital truths inevitably issues in an intellectual lie ; that the last result of reason is scepticism ; that the fruit of the tree of know-ledge produces still, as it did of old, death.' It was the great crisis of his career. Yet in the end he returned with full conviction to the early testimony of the heart and the imagination. There are experienced by all human beings perceptions, affections, emotions, which well up continuously in conscious life— perceptions, affections, emotions beyond analysis as to their source—

> ' High instincts, before which our mortal nature
> Must tremble like a guilty thing surprised.'

Men daily dismiss these instincts as fancies or delusions ; it is easy to discard their suggestions or question their reality, or deny their authority. But for Wordsworth they became the only authentic evidence for the true nature of man and the meaning of human life. He believed that to them should be entrusted the government of the world—

> ' We live by Admiration, Hope, and Love,
> And even as these are well and wisely fixed
> In dignity of being we ascend.'

I

Upon the imagination and affections he was content to lean, admitting that we need

> 'Zeal and the virtue to exist by faith
> As soldiers live by courage ; as by strength
> Of heart, the sailor fights with roaring seas.'

If this be superstition, Wordsworth does not fear superstition. He is prepared to affirm that the Persian presenting sacrifice to moon and stars, the Babylonian tower-builder, or the Greek mother, thankful for her child's return, casting her hair as a thank-offering to the river Cephisus—that these and all other such worshippers were in contact with a reality which swayed and lifted the spirit, and far nearer truth than the apathetic or analytic minds which scorned their delusions.

From the shock given it by the failure of the French Revolution Wordsworth's mind recovered, but recovered slowly. Gradually nature interposed herself between him and his uneasy heart, and he was enabled to recall that which he had lost—

> 'The first diviner influence of this world.'

Nor had his experience been wholly vain. The world of man now claimed him as it had never before claimed him—not indeed on the side of its great achievements or intellectual victories, but on the side of its simple humanity—

> 'The lonely roads
> Were open schools in which I daily read
> With most delight the passions of mankind.
> Whether by words, looks, sighs, or tears revealed ;
> Then saw into the depth of human souls,
> Souls that appear to have no depth at all
> To careless eyes.'

The life of crowded societies might, it was Wordsworth's conviction, sharpen the intelligence, but it tended to dwarf the individual, and he preferred to observe men as they moved and acted and felt and thought in close contact with that nature of which they were a part, which belonged to them as they to it. Such men did not look upon it with an artist's eye, but, like the sailor, who views God's wonders in the great deep, they preserve in their outlook something of the simplicity and freshness of the child. Intellectual insolence is impossible to the Solitary standing in the midst of forces beyond his comprehension, forces flowing out of the infinite and partaking of the infinite. He knows himself the creature of a day. 'There is nothing,' said Wordsworth, ' more worthy of remark in the manners of the inhabitants of these mountains than the tranquillity, I might say indifference, with which they think and talk upon the subject of death.' Never having travelled a great way from nature, they return again willingly, while we, caught up into a noisy atmosphere of distractions and complex artificialities, dread the summons which lays bare the soul and restores it to the bosom of reality. And a study of this virgin and whole-hearted human nature, uncontaminated by commercial rivalries and trivial intercourse, led him to a sense of profound wonder, of inextinguishable reverence for the immensity and sublimity of the human mind. No poet or philosopher before or since has ever stood at gaze like Wordsworth before this spectacle. He seems to brood on the extreme edge of some promontory stretching out into the ocean, lost in a mighty dream of amazement.

> 'Like stout Cortez, when with eagle eyes
> He stared at the Pacific.'

In his study of the heart, therefore, he betook himself, as in his study of nature, to the region where in his view it was unstifled by conventions, untouched by influences which in the populous city distort or deflect its natural movements. The human heart as it came from the hand of God, amid surroundings and forces as they also came from the hand of God, filled him with a sense of infinitude which armed him against all fears—

'All strength—all terror, single or in bands,
That ever was put forth in personal form—
Jehovah—with His thunder, in the choir
Of shouting angels, and the empyreal thrones—
I pass them unalarmed. Not Chaos, not
The darkest pit of lowest Erebus,
Nor aught of blinder vacancy, scooped out
By help of dreams—can breed such fear and awe
As falls upon us often when we look
Into our Minds, into the Mind of Man—
My haunt and the main region of my song.'

Alone of the poets of his age Wordsworth escaped into the light and air after the great disillusionment of the Revolution. Byron was driven into cynicism and despair, Shelley did not indeed abandon his hopes for humanity, but his poetry continually strikes the note of dejection and disappointment. Wordsworth suffered with them, but his strength appears in this, that he emerged from the cloud, and, climbing higher up the mountain, corrected his early perspective and held commerce with vaster presences and the mighty shades of things to come. Near the close of *The Prelude* he describes an almost Apocalyptic vision of the moon above a billowy ocean of cloud, out of which a hundred hills reared their silent crests, and beheld there an

'Emblem of the mind
That feeds upon infinity, that broods
Over the dark abyss, intent to hear
Its voices.'

Perhaps it was passages such as these which Macaulay found 'crazy metaphysics.' But we are here at the centre of Wordsworth's thought ; we have here the highest results of his peculiar method, which fused into a living influence two activities, the power of the object and the power of the mind, making us feel at one and the same moment the beauty and significance of nature, and the majesty and spirituality of man.

If it be desirable—and we are told it is very desirable—to

separate the art of the poet from his religion, the case of Wordsworth is a hard one. For his art is in great measure devoted to a determined exposition of his religion. And if it be desirable to separate art from morality, the case is no less difficult, for he stands obtrusively and deliberately across our path. He desired to be considered as a teacher or as nothing; his mind was unceasingly occupied with moral ideas, he never relinquishes for a moment his sense of duty, he is continually lapsing into the most naked and unashamed didacticism. Here, at least, it will be useless to talk of art for the sake of art. If the matters with which he is endlessly concerned do not interest us, we may close this book.

II

It cannot be overlooked that there is little of natural description in the poetry of Wordsworth. Though one of the most careful observers, awake to the eternal variations, the endless change through which is displayed the life of the external world, there is no attempt to paint these for the physical eye, there is no effort to rival the picture. He was aware 'of the pictorial powerlessness of language,' and the scene is always subordinate to the emotion it excites. The material elements which interested him, the mood in which he approached nature, may be studied in one of his prose works, *A Guide through the District of the Lakes*, a book divided into three sections, the first dealing with *the country as formed by nature*—the shape and colours of the mountains, the valleys, lakes, islands, tarns, woods, wild life, and changing aspects of the sky and climate. The second is concerned with the *aspect of the country as affected by the inhabitants*. Here he notes, for instance, how the cottages scattered over the valleys, or under the hillside, appear as truly a part of the work of nature herself, 'received into the bosom of the living principle of things.' Frequently of the selfsame colour as the native rock, they seem to have grown rather than to have been built. Handed down from generation to generation in the same family, each has received additions as necessity demanded, and in their picturesque variety fit into the landscape around them. Like the rocks from which their materials were quarried, their rough surfaces are stained and weathered, the moss and lichen hang upon their stones and fill their crevices, while in the natural recesses and projections of the walls and the different stages of their roofs the lights and shadows play and blend. In the third section of the book, which deals with *changes, and rules of taste for preventing their bad effects*, Wordsworth maintains that dwellings built amid such scenery should be unobtrusive, if large should partially be hidden, and ought to be of such material, form, and colour as will permit them to be gently incorporated into their surroundings. They cannot rival the features of the natural landscape, and should not attract attention to themselves. An ancient castle on a rock or island may indeed, as owing its existence to the necessities of bygone days, be admitted, but it cannot be imitated with success.

> 'Child of loud-throated war, the mountain stream
>   Roars in thy hearing ; but thy hour of rest
>   Is come, and thou art silent in thy age.'

Observations such as these, free from rhetoric or mysticism, prepare us for the simple integrity of Wordsworth's poetic interpretations, but they prepare us at the same time for a magical treatment of nature akin to that of Turner. Both poet and painter viewed her through the imagination, both associated her with human feeling. And in the sky and cloud effects of Turner we feel, as with Wordsworth, the presence of an open mystery, the mystery of light, bathing the world as in the beginning, itself a revelation, and, like time and space, a bond of visible things. Following Virgil, this poet saw 'universal nature moved by universal mind' ; like 'the good Berkeley,' he believed that the book of nature was written in an intelligible language. The passing shows of bodily being were but the medium through which man 'communed with the glorious universe,' they were the alphabet through which he might spell his way to mysteries hidden, as the splendours of its literature are hidden from the beginner in any language. Blinded by the surprising excellence of the things of sense, as by the radiance of the sun, we may deny that the clear light of reason can hide anything from our eyes, and thus as it were remain ignorant of the immeasurable abyss of stars that only night reveals.

> ' Who could have thought such darkness lay concealed
>   Within thy beams, O Sun ! or who could find,
> Whilst flow'r and leaf and insect stood revealed,
>   That to such countless orbs thou mad'st us blind.'
>   (*Blanco White.*)

Between the mind of man and the universal mind in nature that spoke this intelligible language (with the alphabet of which science is concerned) there existed, and necessarily existed, a secret sympathy. The children of earth, themselves a part of the mighty whole, could not be out of touch with the Cosmos, for they were of it, and through a hundred channels of knowledge truth streamed to them. They were indeed one with all the natural elements, they breathed the air and walked upon the soil, they ate and drank of the kindly fruits, their being was derived and nourished from the same hidden forces. And the crowning wonder was that the Cosmos was intelligible. Nature and man could not be severed ; as his body was a part of her material system, so was his soul a manifestation of the same Divine Being as revealed itself in her order, her sublimity, her beauty. For not otherwise could its beauty, sublimity, or order mean or be anything to him. ' The immortal mind craves objects that endure,' and in the thought of that enduring Power that held the stars in their courses and brought the seasons round there was refuge for human thought which had grown weary on its wing. By entry into the universal life, by vivid realization of his own part in it, Wordsworth believed that he could attain to something of the peace and fullness and dignity and happiness which were there so abundantly displayed. Like his disciple, Arnold, he looked out upon the stars and waters and asked for a portion of their untroubled spirit—

'Unaffrighted by the silence round them,
Undistracted by the sights they see,
These demand not that the things without them
Yield them love, amusement, sympathy.

And with joy the stars perform their shining,
And the sea its long moon-silvered roll ;
For self-poised they live, nor pine with noting
All the fever of some differing soul.'

Beneath the changes, beyond the distractions of every day was thus preserved a foundation for his life. Rooted like a hill flower, amid the uproar and unrest of the storm the mountain was his security. And in so far as it was possible to share in the unchanging and eternal life of nature, which like the ocean beneath its restless surface preserved an immeasurable tranquillity, in so far as he could share in this life he was not only at peace but raised to heights of joyous ecstasy. For besides this eternal strength and divine serenity, nature revealed a widespread happiness, which encompassed and subtly distilled itself into the observer's heart. It might be felt in all her motions, whether of clouds or waters, of bird or beast, insect or flower—

'The budding twigs spread out their fan
To catch the breezy air ;
And I must think, do all I can,
That there was pleasure there.'

In his *Guide to the Lakes* Wordsworth speaks also of the animal life of the district, and of the sounds to which his ear was as delicately susceptible as his eye to the sights. ' The notes of the birds,' he remarks, ' when listened to by the side of broad still waters, or when heard in unison with the murmuring of mountain brooks, have the compass of their power enlarged accordingly.' And again : ' There is also an imaginative influence in the voice of the cuckoo, when that voice has taken possession of a deep mountain valley, very different from anything which can be excited by the same sound in a flat country.' And these observations appear again in his poetry. The bleating of the lamb, when its source is hidden, is finely touched by imagination to a spiritual issue—

> ' The bleating of the lamb, I heard, sent forth
> As if it were the mountain's voice ;
> As if the visible mountain made the cry ;
> The plaintive spirit of the solitude.'

The noise of waters is ever in his ears, from that gentlest of sounds, ' the dripping of the oar suspended,' to that of the torrent,

> ' The mountain flood
> Murmuring from Glaramara's inmost caves.'

He notes the peculiarities in the song of every bird, from the call of the cuckoo to the magpie's chatter—

> ' Over his own sweet voice the stock-dove broods '—
> ' With chiming Tweed the lint-whites sing in chorus.'

The wind sings for him in every key—the roaring sound of the storm in upper air that flows like smoke, the mountain blast that searches the fibres of the caves, ' the bleak music from the old stone wall,' or ' the pointed crags that into music touch the passing wind.' It is perhaps not possible to be sensitive in this way to sounds without also feeling the power of silence. Few things are more impressive than a day of perfect stillness among the mountains or by the sea—

> ' When even the motion of an angel's wing
> Would interrupt the intense tranquillity
> Of silent hills, and more than silent sky.'

To be surrounded by mighty presences which are silent in

their strength is a more heart-searching experience than when they are full of their own proper voices, when the wind sweeps the earth and vexes the waters. And some of Wordsworth's most haunting lines are associated with the power of nature's quiet—

> 'The silence that is in the starry sky,
> The sleep that is among the lonely hills.'

Nor does he fail to note, as in his sonnet on Westminster Bridge, the same presence of quiet, where from the busy traffic of a great city usually arises the ocean-like far-extending roar of many contending sounds, and the peace is deeper than the peace of the fields where noises never come.

Poetry, said Wordsworth, 'is an acknowledgment of the beauty of the universe,' and 'a homage paid to the native and naked dignity of man.' If we turn from the poems which make this acknowledgment to those which pay this homage, we find that the human type which chiefly interested him partook most fully of the qualities that belonged to the larger universal life. He loved best the characters which fitted, like their own mountain cottages, most sweetly and naturally into the great plan of things. Take *The Leech Gatherer*. The poem opens with the lines—

> 'There was a roaring in the wind all night,
> The rain came heavily and fell in floods'—

But after the night of storm came a morning of calm and sunshine, and all things that love the sun were abroad and rejoicing. The birds, the hares, were busy; the grass was bright with raindrops, the air filled with the pleasant noise of waters. Such a morning uplifts the heart and spirits, and the poet felt the prevailing happiness rising in his own heart. But, as often happens, in the very moment of his greatest natural joy there fastened upon him a dim sadness and blind uneasy thoughts. It was a day to rejoice, but he thought of others, days of 'solitude, pain of heart, distress and poverty.' He thought and could not dismiss the thought, that many had been the poets to whom life had been unkind. And in this mood as he crossed the moor, beside a pool,

> 'I saw a man before me unawares,
>   The oldest man he seemed that ever wore grey hairs'

—a man bent double with age, who supported himself on a long staff.

> 'Upon the margin of that moorish flood,
>   Motionless as a cloud, the old man stood
>   That heareth not the loud winds when they call
>   And moveth all together, if it move at all.'

In conversation Wordsworth learns that the old man is a leech-gatherer, that he is the only survivor of his family, that his wife and children are dead, and that he supports himself with difficulty, for leeches are now scarce where he was accustomed to find them. Yet he retains his cheerfulness. Old and solitary, supporting existence meagrely by toilsome labour on the bleak mountain moor, he bears his burden unsubdued in spirit and wears a contented brow. Wordsworth finds his story hard to believe ; he thinks of

> 'The fear that kills
>   And hope that is unwilling to be fed,
>   Cold, pain, and labour, and all fleshly ills,
>   And mighty poets in their misery dead.'

Perplexed he asks again, 'How is it that you live, and what is it you do ?' With a smile the old man repeats his tale, and then in stately fashion turns the conversation to other themes. While he talks Wordsworth is troubled. In his mind's eye he seems

> 'To see him pace
>   About the weary moors continually
>   Wandering about alone and silently.'

And then the fortitude and native spirit, the grandeur and simplicity of the situation force themselves upon him, and compel him to passionate admiration—

> 'I could have laughed myself to scorn to find
> In that decrepit man so firm a mind.
> "God," said I, "be my help and stay secure :
> I'll think of the leech-gatherer on the lonely moor !"'

Thus in the poem we are made to feel that the solitary old man upon the moor is a real part of his surroundings, in harmony with the whole, like a huge stone upon an eminence, or a motionless cloud upon the horizon. But more than this, it would appear that his calmness and courage, his strength of heart, are somehow derived from the nature with which he is in such close communion, and are not unworthy of her. He seems, like a star, to move with untroubled acquiescence in his appointed orbit.

But it may be asked, does not the poet overlook the merci-lessness or at least the indifference of the mighty powers within whose jurisdiction our life is cast, the suffering and pain which are so obviously present in the life of sentient things ? Only the cheapest optimism can ignore the elements of discord and distress no less apparent in the world than beauty and order. Wordsworth was profoundly conscious of these elements. He had felt

> 'The heavy and the weary weight
> Of all this unintelligible world.'

He was aware that

> 'The clouds that gather round the setting sun
> Do take a sober colouring from the eye
> That hath kept watch o'er man's mortality.'

No more trustworthy evidence that his confidence and courage were not due to blindness can be given than the poem entitled *Hart-Leap Well*, where the story is told of a hart which, after a desperate chase of thirteen hours, reached at last in three frantic leaps a spring on the hillside, and was found by the huntsman there, stretched dead by its brink. Wordsworth thinks of the poor creature as a member of the great family of living things, and feels for its sufferings. He ponders what must have been its thoughts, and what causes led it to make so desperate an effort to reach the fountain where it died.

> 'Here on the grass, perhaps, asleep he sank,
> Lulled by the fountain in the summer tide,
> This water was perhaps the first he drank
> When he had wandered from his mother's side.'

The pity of it comes home to him, he feels it as he would feel the pang of human suffering and fear, and yet enunciates his often expressed conviction—

> 'This Beast not unobserved by Nature fell ;
> His death was mourned by sympathy divine.'

He tells us that

> 'The Being that is in the clouds and air,
> That is in the green leaves among the groves,
> Maintains a deep and reverential care
> For the unoffending creatures that He loves.'

He clings to this faith, though he is aware that such ravages are apparently endless and soon forgotten, and that

> 'Nature in due course of time, once more
> Shall here put on her beauty and her bloom.'

The creed may be difficult of acceptance, but we are sure of two things—Wordsworth meant what he said, he is expressing an absolute conviction, and it is a conviction which was nourished not in ignorance, but after he had faced the facts in his severe uncompromising way. So that his proposal to us in the face of the anxieties, the disquietudes, the sorrows and dis-

tractions of life seems to differ fundamentally from that of most
poets. He never counsels retreat, he does not ask us to forget
ourselves amid the delicate traceries, the dim beauty of the
Palace of Art, but rather to remember ourselves, and, in answer
to all enigmas, trust the witness of our deepest instincts and
seek within the soul an inner harmony of powers and feelings.
He himself attained that inner harmony, and in the room of
Byron's combative mood, or the dreaming mood of Keats or
Coleridge, we have his magnificent equanimity, his resolution
and his unconquerable hope. Perhaps, as Goethe said of
Winckelmann, 'One learns nothing from him, but one becomes
something.'

> 'We feel that we are greater than we know.'

III

There seems to be a curious almost an inhuman, insensibility,
in the poetry of Wordsworth to that eternal flux of things which
seems to make of the life of man, its sorrows and its joys, a trivial
accident. The sentiment most common in poetry, the sentiment of sad reflection that ' beauty passes like a dream,' is a
note rarely if ever struck by him. His thesis is the antithesis
of the cry we hear from the poets of all ages—the cry heard in
the *Ballad of Dead Ladies*—

> 'Tell me now in what hidden way is
>   Lady Flora, the lovely Roman?
> Where's Hipparchia, and where is Thaïs,
>   Neither of them the fairer woman?
> Where is Echo, beheld of no man,
>   Only heard on river and mere—
> She whose beauty was more than human?
> But where are the snows of yester-year?'

Of this sentiment, so powerful a strain in human history,
there is in Wordsworth hardly a trace. And there is also a
strange absence of the similar strain which meets us so often

in the poetry of Keats and Tennyson,—' the passion of the past,' that irresistible summons to admiration and amazement before heroic deeds and lovely faces of days long dead, thoughts of men and women we can never know, triumphs we can never share, palaces and cities we can never behold. To the glamour and the mystery of these things Wordsworth was indifferent, the thread of this romance was never woven into the fabric of his verse. It was his wish not to describe but to interpret life. And nothing is perhaps more strange and admirable than the dogged persistence, let us call it, with which he clings to the simpler elements of human life, his persevering refusal to select heroic themes. He avoids in his building all the choice marbles and selected woods, which, apart from its architecture, may be employed to beautify the Palace of Poetry. Wordsworth draws next to nothing from the storehouse of classical myth or renaissance fancy or mediæval romance. He takes human nature in its least inspiring moments, in its least moving episodes, in its very humblest representatives. He tells no tales of lovers, adorns no exciting themes, his plots are totally devoid of stirring incidents. 'How insignificant a thing,' he said, 'does personal prowess appear compared with the fortitude of patience and heroic martyrdom,' and in a single sentence displays his preferences. He admired most the least obvious virtues, and chiefly the power of resolute endurance. Others might celebrate heroic exploits, adventurous voyage and romantic quest, great doings which demand nerve and spirit and the fresh-heartedness of youth. Wordsworth believed that the spiritual nature of man was best exhibited in its power to bear suffering through weary nights and days, in its power of preserving, amid all buffetings of fortune, serenity of mind and soul, when self-sustained they were

> 'Held above
> The infirmities of mortal love ;
> Undaunted, lofty, calm and stable,
> And awfully impenetrable.'

He would, it appears, have us confess that not in its external trappings but in its simple essentials human life is significant, and would convert us to a spiritual creed not by dwelling upon the pomp and chivalry of human history, but on its weak and poor and often miserable estate. He declines as a poet the attempt to outsoar the humanities. This is the first principle by which he is governed. The content of his poetry is determined by it. And the form of his poetry is governed by a similar principle. Wordsworth almost perversely refuses to employ language for decorative purposes. He is innocent of the tricks of the trade, he is nothing of a rhetorician. He appears not to understand, or did not deign to use, the arts by which the absence of thought or inspiration can be disguised. Poets like Keats or Tennyson, when they have little to say, say it all the more eloquently. They realize their weakness and cover it magnificently. It is never so with Wordsworth. His undeviating aim is to find the exact words which fit the thing— not golden words, such as are the common inheritance of the poets, but 'simple and unelaborated expressions.' 'There will be found in these volumes,' he wrote, 'little of what is usually called poetic diction ; as much pains has been taken to avoid it as is ordinarily taken to produce it.'

And in his best moments he has this in common with Shakespeare, that he is without mannerism. Take lines like these—

> 'Truth fails not ; but her outward forms that bear
> The longest date do melt like frosty rime
> That in the morning whitened hill and plain
> And is no more ; drop like the tower sublime
> Of yesterday, which royally did wear
> His crown of weeds, but could not even sustain
> Some casual shout that broke the silent air
> Or the unimaginable touch of Time.'

Here, as in a hundred other passages, the absence of effort, the limpid clearness and exactness of phrase, the reserve, almost austerity of the diction challenge comparison with anything in the language. ' The expression,' as Arnold said, ' may often be called bald, but it is bald as the bare mountain-tops are bald, with a baldness which is full of grandeur.' What gives to his poetry its unique and fascinating power ? The fact that it can dispense with ornament ; the very colourlessness of the expression is its strength. In the chastity of his phrase we mark an antique quality. Sculpturesque rather than picturesque, Greek rather than Gothic, it impresses by the naked simplicity of conception, the beauty of outline, by its form and spacing, by its proportions and adjustments. Richness and wealth of colour, complexity of detail, none can deny the charm of these things, but how frequently they serve to cover the absence of design, and to withdraw the mind from the central idea. Wordsworth's poetry is a pillar which marks the true highway of Art, to which highway, from all its recoils and excursions, after all its temporary revolts and worship of new creeds in high places, it must ever return, content to find its guidance in principles tried and age-long. To their austerity, their splendid economy of phrase, his sonnets particularly owe their far-shining pre-eminence. The sonnet presented the limitations which saved Wordsworth from his faults of prolixity and tediousness, for there was no room for prologue or exordium. And in the best of them every line is like a column in the portico of a Doric temple, upon which the eye does not rest for itself, since it is merged in the pure and massive breadth of the whole design.

It is sometimes difficult to believe that the *dramatis personæ* of Wordsworth's poems are real men and women and not wandering spirits, who, amid the solemn mountains and the solitary valleys they frequent, are met by the poet and by some magic incantation bidden to stand and speak. They seem to be creatures of the elements, and seem so partly, indeed, because they are usually country folk, invested with a certain loneliness. Wordsworth's canvas is never crowded. He approaches his subject slowly, and we seem to see the people in whom he would interest us, at first, a great way off. As we advance, the figures become sharper and clearer until the last detail is grasped. And in his delineation of the domestic affections he isolates the emotion, and thus allows it, freed from all conflicting feelings, to sink into the heart—the emotion of the parent, it may be, as in *Michael*, or of fraternal love as in *The Brothers* ; but he is never concerned with a complicated or abnormal situation. The passions with which he deals are invariably simple and invariably natural. Questions of casuistry do not arise as in *Hamlet*, nor do we lean over precipices of hatred or revenge as in *Macbeth*, nor enter the torturing fields of jealousy and malignity as in *Othello*. These reaches were beyond Wordsworth. Moral distortions, fierce mental conflict, spiritual degradation, crime, the march of the avenging Furies, were out of his range. Nor could he figure for himself the inter-related life of a great society, groups of persons with clashing interests and purposes, the wars and tumults of a crowded stage. Unlike Coleridge, again, though in a sense a philosophical poet, he cared nothing for the distinctions of ' subject ' and ' object ' ; he would have regarded the dialectic of Hegel as the merest ploughing of the sand. To the imagination he looked rather than the reason, to the imagination—and this is strange and of his essence—as a practical guide to life. To harness Pegasus to an earthly chariot, to compel the imagination to serve actual human needs, such was his ambitious programme. Poetry for poetry's sake was not Wordsworth's motto. Rather it was poetry for life's sake. He looked upon it as a means whereby men might be touched to finer issues, through which the spirit might be familiarized with its own truest and best moods, and might dwell longer in the atmosphere of its highest moments. His philosophy condescends to ask for no justification, leans upon no buttresses provided by the logical faculty, but towers above the clouds of controversy, and, like some virgin peak, keeps its fraternal vigil with the stars.

' Other poetry,' said Leslie Stephen, ' becomes trifling when
we are making our inevitable passages through the Valley
of the Shadow of Death. Wordsworth's alone retains its
power. We love him the more as we grow older and become more deeply influenced with the sadness and seriousness
of life ; we are apt to grow weary of his rivals when we have
finally quitted the regions of youthful enchantment.'

IV

When we come to *The Excursion* we come to the severest
test of discipleship. ' Didactic poetry is my abhorrence,' said
Shelley ; and *The Excursion* is wholly didactic. The author is
here exposed to the attack of his besetting sins—a tendency to
prolixity and a tendency to preaching. He was already, when
engaged upon it, past the generous period of his youth, inclined
towards a hard and legal form of morality, and rarely visited
by the passionate magnanimity of his early self. The fire of
his genius was beginning to burn low. The maturer experience
of life, the sanity which takes the place of the enthusiasm, the
serenity which is as appropriate to age as heat and fervour to
youth, were in some degree compensations ; but none the less
The Excursion, when we apply the most rigorous canons of
poetry—and it would be mere impertinence to apply to Wordsworth any but the most rigorous canons—is only acceptable, as
are also, for example, his *Ecclesiastical Sonnets*, in passages. And
it will never be acceptable to those readers and critics who
insist that poetry shall be a place of dreams, a country of delightful illusions. Readers and critics who belong to the school of
Rossetti and Morris find in poetry, or deny that it is poetry,
a charm to bring about forgetfulness of the weight and weariness
of life. For them it is an incantation to be crooned over till
the actual world, a world of trouble and disquiet, recedes into
the distance and its harsh noises are no longer heard. They allow
to Wordsworth's lyrical poems a magical singing quality, which

lulls the heart to rest, but they can meet no trace of it in the bulk of his longer works. And so the name Wordsworthian has almost come to be synonymous with a hater of true poetry, or at least with a reader who knows nothing of its true meaning and feeds upon ' objects, arts, and imitations.' It may well be that those who read a poet for his philosophy, social or moral, seek first the things that are not of the spirit. But it may also be doubted whether those who seek in poetry a stimulant or narcotic merely, who regard it as the wine rather than the bread of life, are not equally far from the centre as its dullest votaries.

In *The Excursion* Wordsworth ventures anew upon the ground of an ancient controversy. The Cosmos is or must in the end prove rational, morally intelligible—that is one position : it is, and never will be anything but irrational, and bitter-sweet at best, is the other and antithetical position. In the persons of the Wanderer and the Solitary the debate is presented and the poet's matured view of human life and society elaborately set forth. It is important to note that *The Excursion* is not a work of Wordsworth's revolutionary but of his later conservative period. He was no longer anxious for the dreadful winds of change to pass over the face of the world. Its existing institutions, its stratification, its fashions he accepted as part of the natural order, as representing on the whole the best that man had hitherto thought and willed. Nor indeed was Wordsworth at any time a zealous architect in social fabrics. The splendid visions of his youth rarely if ever condescended to detail, nor had his mind projected more than the outline of a free commonwealth, of which the internal fittings and adjustments were to be left to the future. Like Browning, his primary interest was with the individual soul. He found a soul when it was supposed barely to have emerged into existence, among the simplest and humblest of mankind. And, like Browning, he endeavoured to surprise it at great crises in its history, under the stress of emotion, and believed, like him, that in its native hardihood it was equal to all the buffetings of time and circumstance, and stronger than its most evil star. With Shelley and with Tennyson the centre of interest is to be sought in the race rather than in the individual. They look out over the untravelled sea, and expect for men a heaven upon earth in the great coming days when the forces of nature have been subdued and the world transformed into a community of brothers and philosophers. Browning and Wordsworth rise far indeed above such mundane ideals as a ' Parliament of man, a federation of the world,' nor for them was there any inspiration to be drawn from the purple prospect of a Positivist Paradise.

In the first book of *The Excursion* the poet meets the Wanderer, a pedlar, who in the course of his journeys has meditated deeply on the mysteries, the joys and sorrows of human life, who has lived among the villages in the country-side and is himself also a poet, a late representative of the minstrel, who can sing ' old songs, the product of his native hills.' The Wanderer is the cheerful philosopher who has found life worth living, and represents in large measure the point of view taken by Wordsworth himself. Such a life, that of the pedlar, has always, he tells us, appealed to him—

' Had I been born in a class which would have deprived me of what is called a liberal education, it is not unlikely that, being strong in body, I should have taken to a way of life such as that in which my Pedlar passed the greater part of his days. At all events, I am here called upon to acknowledge that the character I have represented in his person is chiefly an idea of what I fancied my own character might have become in his circumstances.'

The Solitary, who carries on the debate with the Wanderer, is represented as one who has suffered greatly and felt the disillusionment of life. Fate had been unkind, he lost his wife and family, and the hopes for the human race he had cherished went down with the wreck of principles after the French

Revolution. He is no longer convinced of the worth of life, and with his scepticism mingles a certain irony which points his discourse. In the effort to restore the Solitary to a faith in the Divine ordering of the world, the Wanderer draws upon his own experiences, and relates some simple and pathetic annals of the poor, the stories of those who sleep in the churchyard among the mountains. *The Excursion* is not a great poem, it is not even a great philosophical treatise, but it is great in passages. When we read of

> ' Towers begirt
> With battlements that on their restless fronts
> Bore stars,'

or

> ' 'Tis a thing impossible to frame
> Conceptions equal to the soul's desires :
> And the most difficult of tasks to keep
> Heights which the soul is competent to gain,'

we know that to this poet belonged something of the grandeur of Milton, something of the insight of Browning. And there are verses in which he rises to his own proper stature, and we know him for one of the giants—

> ' Such was the boy—but for the growing youth
> What soul was his, when, from the naked top
> Of some bold headland, he beheld the sun
> Rise up and bathe the world in light ! He looked—
> Ocean and earth, the solid frame of earth
> And ocean's liquid mass, in gladness lay
> Beneath him : far and wide the clouds were touched
> And in their silent faces could be read
> Unutterable love. Sound needed none,
> Nor any voice of joy ; his spirit drank
> The spectacle ; sensation, soul, and form
> All melted into him ; they swallowed up
> His animal being ; in them did he live,
> And by them did he live : they were his life.

In such access of mind, in such high hour
Of visitation from the living God,
Thought was not ; in enjoyment it expired.
No thanks he breathed, he proffered no request :
Rapt into still communion that transcends
The imperfect offices of prayer and praise,
His mind was a thanksgiving to the Power
That made him ; it was blessedness and love !'

The characters in *The Excursion* are plain men, and their speech is plain. Wordsworth, as I have said, discarded the heroic subject, the decorative manner, the familiar associations of poetry, and adventured upon themes almost grovelling in their common simplicity, sometimes indeed ludicrously trivial. But whether it be the ordinary sights and sounds, the cuckoo's cry, or the bed of daffodils, whether it be the story of the wicked pedlar converted through the instrumentality of an ill-treated donkey, or that of an old leech-gatherer picking up a precarious living on a lonely moor, he rarely fails to draw the mind into sympathy with the world of supernatural powers, and leave it persuaded of the spiritual life. As with Socrates, we talk to this plain man about ordinary matters as in a conversational key—the matters of the fields and streets, the bazaars and market-places—we feel ourselves safe in his company. Here is a man of common sense, we say, without superstitions, who under-stands how little poetry and philosophy have to do with life. But before we are aware of the processes, we are suddenly betrayed into admissions of a transcendental character. Men like Socrates and Wordsworth, by reason of this method of theirs, the method which begins with things acknowledged and vulgar, are the most dangerous of all the enemies of materialism. The materialistic creed has little to dread from the poets of art, from *Atalanta in Calydon* or *The Earthly Paradise*. Such poetry fears vulgarity, and beats a retreat to the island in the river where we can make music to ourselves and forget the city's din. But it is at heart persuaded of the creed it would escape. Nor has materialism much to fear from religion which bids us forsake the world and the flesh, calling by evil names the things that men have ever found delightful. Nor will it suffer defeat from the philosophers who move in the sphere of abstractions amid a whirl of words, forgetful that it is blood that flows in our veins and that the things of sense hold and surround us with a hoop of steel. But a poetry or a religion or a philosophy which takes its stand upon the beggarly elements of our common nature, with which pain is pain, and joy joy, for which starvation and thirst, poverty and wealth, rank, childhood and manhood, age and youth, are real things, which makes no attempt to juggle us into the doctrine that evil is an appearance, or pain an aspect of pleasure, or wealth and rank less desirable than misery and starvation—the poetry or religion or philosophy which is able to look facts in the face and at the same time persuade us that our true life is greater than we know, and can open for us sudden and strange vistas until, through a gathering sense of awe and mystery, we think we know

> 'The hills where our life rose
> And the sea where it goes'

—such a poetry or religion or philosophy will enable men, as Plato said, to live dear to one another and to the gods, while it prepares them for the pilgrimage of a thousand years which awaits the soul.

Scott[1]

It was in September 1832 that Scott died; 1932 is close upon us. The century which divides us from the most famous of Scotsmen draws to a close. A writer, it has been said, is a classic who is read 100 years after his death. Well, how does Scott now stand? He is an immortal, no doubt. But how many of the immortals are names to us, names and nothing more than names! Is Scott still veritably alive, has he anything of consequence to say to us, after a century the most revolutionary, I suppose, in human history, so crowded with momentous events, with startling discoveries, that it has transformed the very conditions of existence? For we might well ask, 'Do we, indeed, inhabit the same world as that in which he lived and wrote?'

Looking back upon it, how leisurely seems the life of a hundred years ago, how sleepy and rural! How large and half-explored was then the world, how small the cities, and uncongested the traffic! The astronomers have since enlarged the heavens, but the electricians have contracted the earth. Anxiously, for example, as you might desire speed in those days, speed in our sense of the word was unobtainable. Dr. Johnson's idea of supreme earthly felicity was to drive rapidly in a chaise with a pretty lady. How happy, then, should we be who can drive with the lady of our choice at a pace which would have taken the old moralist's breath away. Scott, a generation later than Johnson, never sent a telegram, or even bought a railway ticket. When he and his friends travelled they took coach, or rode on horseback, rarely exceeding the decent limit of eight or ten miles an hour. India was then a two months' voyage. Our trains attain sixty or seventy,

---

[1] Address at the annual dinner of the Edinburgh Sir Walter Scott Club, on 27th November 1931.

our aeroplanes three to four hundred miles an hour. Scott
took six or seven days to reach London from Edinburgh. The
journey from London to Rome and back has recently been
accomplished in a day. Scott and his friends were unacquainted
with such admirable things as postage stamps or policemen,
and the idea of income tax was then no more than a pleasant
novelty. The most inspired prophets of that time, not so very
long ago, hardly more than the span of a single life, had not
foretold, so limited is human foresight, the coming of motor
cars, or picture houses, or telephones, or aeroplanes. Not one
of them, for all their wisdom, had even dreamt of wireless or
electric light. They were not aware, poor souls, that space
was curved. I am not sure that they had ever heard of the
ether. But that was not, perhaps, of much account, for there
are persistent rumours that it is dead, murdered in cold blood
by the mathematicians. It was Faraday's electro-magnetic
work, in the years between 1830 and 1840, that transformed
the whole fabric of our existence. We have certainly travelled
fast and far since Sir Walter's day. A revolution has taken
place in our ways of living.

Yet it is not this revolution which divides us, as any one
can see we are divided, from the times and from the thought
of Scott. After all these wonderful toys—and they are wonderful, our aeroplanes and our wireless—have effected no
alteration in our hearts, have not altered in a single fibre the
structure of our souls. If the millennium has arrived it is only
the millennium of machinery. There is nothing fundamental
in changes such as these, nothing in them to chill our sympathies with Scott's creations, nothing to prevent our sharing
to the full all his beliefs, all his loves, all his admirations. Yet
it is transparently clear that in fact we no longer do so, that
his ways of thinking are no longer our ways of thinking. A
great breach with belief and tradition has taken place. The
externals of life have changed, manners have changed. Yes,
but most of all minds have changed. No one who reflects

for a moment but is aware that Scott's vision is not our vision. We think in different dimensions, we employ different concepts —that hard-worked term, evolution, for example. We look out upon the world with very different eyes, and it cannot be denied with saddened and disillusioned eyes. Somehow the sky has darkened, and our mental landscape is, by contrast, sullen and overcast.

What then has happened ? To say all in a word, Scott was a Romantic and a hero-worshipper, and we have ceased to be Romantics and hero-worshippers. He was a poet. We have lost faith in poets, and transferred our allegiance from poetry to science. He looked out upon the great panorama of human life with unconcealed delight : we regard it with anxiety and misgiving. He was quick to love, to believe, and to admire. We are sceptical and critical, quick to doubt, to decry, and to defame. He came before Darwin and Freud, and was persuaded of man's kinship with the angels. We are persuaded of his much closer kinship with the animals. He thought nobly of the soul. 'The soul ?' we ask, 'What is that ?' Honour and chivalry were for him words of profound depth and meaning. Words such as these occur but seldom in the vocabulary of modern authors. They have dropped out of use. He praised glory and patriotism. With us glory and patriotism are both under suspicion. He had a passion for soldiers and valiant deeds. 'I, Walter Scott of Abbotsford, a poor scholar, no soldier, but a soldier's lover,' he called himself. He never doubted that death in his country's cause was the noblest death a man could die. 'Never let me hear that brave blood has been shed in vain,' he cried, 'it sends an imperious challenge down through all the generations.' We speak of wars and battles with loathing, and declare the lives they take as wholly thrown away, as madly wasted. One might have imagined that at least the magnificent heroism, the fortitude, the self-sacrifice displayed by men of all nations in the late war would have inspired modern writers. Not so, they have no eyes for them, do not rejoice in them or praise them, but are plunged in the deepest dejection.

Since, then, Scott's sentiments and ideas are no longer ours, since we have parted from them, has he any living force to-day? Is he anything more than the shadow of a great name?

Well, for my part I believe that for his ideas, his ways of thought, there is still an audience, and still something to be said. At least—and it is not an altogether negligible matter—the world he lived in, and whose ways of thought he shared, seems to have been a happier and more hopeful world. We have captured speed on earth, air, and sea, but not happiness. It is a remarkable fact, however you propose to explain it, that despite all the splendid achievements of science, a great restlessness prevails. More than that, disappointment with life, aversion from life, even hatred of it, are plainly written, so that all may read, in the world-wide discontents, in the books, in the spirit and temper of our times. Our century ponders, like Hamlet, with the skull in his hand. Do not let us imagine that all this is merely the aftermath of the war. There is no exit that way. For you may see it clearly enough if side by side with the novels and poems of Scott you place the works of Tolstoy, or the novels and poems of one of the most popular of our pre-war authors, Thomas Hardy. In his writings there is not much cheerfulness abroad. They do not sparkle with the joy of life. Whatever their genius and merits, no one, I suppose, will claim that they are charged with happiness and hopefulness, that they increase our love of existence or desire for it. Contrast Scott, who searched the annals of his country, the annals of mankind, for deeds to admire and characters to praise. For him the long avenues of history were crowded with heroic figures, lined with the statues of illustrious men and noble women, examples to be revered and imitated. It was his happiness and pride to be the guide of ardent youth through the fields of fame, the inspiring scenes, the gallant deeds and splendid enterprises. Our modern writers prefer to dwell upon the gloomier prospects. They appear to share the opinion of Hobbes, that human life may best be described as ' nasty, brutish, and short.' You may take that view, but it digs the grave of poetry. To make poetry of it is wholly impossible.

> ' Not here, O Apollo !
> Are haunts meet for thee.'

It would seem that only what is ugly is true, and beauty another name for falsehood. Wisdom consists in thinking meanly of ourselves and of human life. How many of our authors write, to borrow a phrase of Goethe's, ' as if they were ill, and the whole world a hospital.' The cupboards have been ransacked for their skeletons, for which they exhibit a peculiar affection. No wonder, perhaps, for to discover a skeleton to-day is to discover a gold-mine. If I could prove to you this evening that Scott was a drug-addict, or the father of illegitimate children, my fortune would be made. I should awake to-morrow to find myself famous. But there are no skeletons in Scott's cupboard, and I must content myself with academic obscurity. For the younger generation, the new-comers on the stage of time, I cannot discover that our age has any very inspiriting tidings. The babies are met with bad news. Nature, fortunately, has some kindliness in her disposition, and has made youth the season of hope. But I for one am glad that I did not begin life with the information that it was a bad business, a vale of tears, a losing battle, leading to nothing but the grave. Scott knew what a losing battle was, better than most, but he was a soldier, a fighter, not, like so many of our contemporaries, a defeatist. Who can read his ' Journal ' without consuming admiration, without a movement of the heart towards its author ? ' I shall do my duty. Do what is right, come what may.'—' I will never relax my labour.'—' I will die with honour.' Scott had something more than genius, he ha character. With us pity for ourselves, pity for our neigh has drowned all the other virtues. But the sorrows of the world are not new sorrows, and men before our time have endured them. More even than his talents, I admire in Scott the iron in his soul, the 'No Surrender' resolution, like that of which he wrote in his description of Flodden, where

> 'The stubborn spearmen still made good
> The dark impenetrable wood,
> Each stepping where his comrade stood
> The instant that he fell.'

Yes, Scott was a Romantic, heroic himself and a hero-worshipper. Not yet a century has passed, and where are now his poetic outlook, his eager high-hearted enthusiasms, his pride in human nature? Not yet a century, and how many of the old faiths, the ancient loyalties survive? The sunshine has left the fields, and romance lies dead. Are we to congratulate ourselves?

Let us not be unduly pessimistic. There have been gains as well as losses. If our age is truly engaged, as it asserts and proclaims, in a battle against shams, if it demands everywhere and at all times the truth, if it refuses any longer to look at life through rose-coloured glasses—these decisions are not to be deplored. It is not to be deplored that we have set our faces against senseless slaughter, against falsehood, and cant, and hypocrisy.

But Truth is a mysterious lady. No one knows where she li   o one has yet discovered her palace, nor even the lodge   And as matters now stand, we find ourselves in   ation.

                          an age of poetry, the age of Byron and Shelley,
                          and Coleridge, and Keats. He represents a
                          a very ancient doctrine—the support and
                          human race since the dawn of time—the
                          poetry. The succeeding age believed it
                          transferred its allegiance to a new faith

and new doctrine. Reason and science, not poetry, were to lead the coming generations to truth and happiness. Here at last, we were told, we stood upon sure foundations, upon solid rock. Yet somehow, such is the strange situation, we have not found happiness, and even truth seems to have escaped our grasp. For to the discerning eye it is clear that, despite all her victories, science stands to-day bewildered before her own conclusions, and reason is ill at ease upon her imperial throne.

Well, you may ask, whither does this argument lead, and what has this to do with Scott? It leads, I think, to the conclusion that the old-fashioned among us, the lovers of poetry and the lovers of Scott, need not forsake their old loves, their old loyalties. I have read a good deal of contemporary literature, philosophy, and science, and I confess to you that I have found nothing better than Scott gave us, no better literature, no more secure or solid creed than his, no better example than his of how life should be lived. I think him a wiser and better friend for old and young than any writer of our own time. For my part, too, I am still convinced that poetry goes nearer the heart of things, goes deeper than logic, and that the language of poetry is better suited to interpret life for us than the language of science. Human problems are not to be solved by machinery, by algebra or decimals. We live by the inner light. Take away from the world its romance and its poetry, the belief that we are greater than we know, and may become greater than we are, which is the essence of the poetic creed, and you take away hope, you 'take the Spring out of the year.' For this creed Scott stood—still stands. He is of the noble army in whose company we experience a lifting, not a sinking of the heart. It was said of Wellington in the Peninsula that in moments of doubt and anxiety the sight of his nose was worth ten thousand men. Scott, too, had a lion's heart. He has encouragement in his voice and presence. He stirs the heart like a trumpet.

But, it may be objected, even if what you say is t

half true, Scott is not, after all, of the first order of poets, not among the great spiritual leaders of mankind. He was no thinker. He had a boyish mind, and wrote boys' books. He is not merely out of fashion, he is out of date. We have outgrown him. It may be objected, too, that he is no trustworthy historian, that his antiquarianism is all false, that the past he describes for us is a past that never was a present. I am not concerned to claim for him divine honours. He himself knew very well that greater minds than his own had appeared in the world, and was properly impatient when overpraised. 'The blockheads talk of my being like Shakespeare,' he wrote, 'not fit to tie his brogues.' But when all is said, I remain a stubborn and impenitent admirer of the man. For some reason character is, alas, often divorced from talent. But when I am inclined to dwell upon his literary defects, I think of the man, and he rises once more to his heroic stature. And when all is said that can be said in his dispraise, I still approach with reverence a writer in the first rank of creative genius, who has given happiness to millions, who has nations for his audience, and readers in every continent. When I contemplate his vast canvas, the breadth, the opulence, the power, he still seems to me a Triton among the minnows ; I ask ' Where are now his peers ? ' It was said of Plato that ' he took his view of everything as from a lofty rock.' And with Scott, too, we ascend an eminence to share his wide, genial, affectionate survey of all things human. The world to-day is full of clever writers, im— cleverer than Scott. He was not, thank God, a He has no witticisms. Yet not a man of them tter can bend as he bent the great bow, the bow hen I ponder it I cannot avoid the conviction uch talent as the great soul that makes the

ortal, and had his faults, his weaknesses. taste, there is much beside cleverness Unlike Mr. Bernard Shaw, for example, he had a poor opinion of his own performances. ' You know,' he said to Lockhart, ' you know I don't care a damn for anything I write.' Modesty is not a modern failing, but personally I do not find it disagreeable. Then again, he had a respect and affection for his forebears, whereas the authors of our time are constrained to deal faithfully with the faults of their fathers and the follies of the mothers who bore them. Every one to his taste.

There are other items in the indictment against Scott. ' He wrote nothing,' it was said and repeated, ' that appealed to the immortal part of man.' Then, in the name of all the saints at once, I ask, ' What is immortal in us ? ' Of all the charges against him this is the charge to which I listen with the keenest impatience. As if the best in us could be aroused only by sermons ! As if the breathing earth, the hills and streams, the movements of the human heart, of which he wrote, as if his sweetness of temper, his magnanimity, his fortitude, his transparent, deep affections, which shine through every sentence, were not divine ! For my part I count him among the heavenly influences.

There are superior persons among us who smile if you speak of Scott as a poet. To be sure, he is intelligible, and that goes grievously against him. He is also objective, unequipped with any knowledge of psycho-analysis or the ductless glands. He sees men and things as they appear, and not as the learned doctors tell us they really are.

He judges men by their actions, and things by the impression they make upon our senses. And how else are we to judge them ? And how else in practice do the theorists judge them ? Nature and the soul have, indeed, their hidden depths. But till exploration has gone vastly further than it has gone, or, I venture to think, will ever go, the actions of men and the impression made by things upon our senses will remain, and cannot but remain our daily standards and measurements. There is a pernicious habit abroad in criticism of judging artists

by what they have not done, or by the ideals of other ages
than their own. Why demand the qualities of Milton in
Shelley, of Beethoven in Scarlatti, or of Rembrandt in Raphael?
Let us take the best we can get anywhere and be thankful.
And as for poetry, there are, I venture to believe, few poets
even now, however superior, who would not gladly accept the
authorship of Scott's lyrics. If they will not have them, let
me be their author, and any one who pleases may have the
better and profounder poems of to-day.

What else remains on the charge sheet? The historians have
discovered that Scott's pictures of the past are inaccurate. The
high-powered microscope of modern research has revealed his
errors. An earlier, and far more significant, discovery had,
however, been made by Scott himself, the discovery of the
human values of history. He discerned that it was not a matter
of curious ruins and musty parchments, a desolate, waste land,
but an inhabited country. He first peopled the past with men
and women like ourselves, and made it live, as the pedants
have never made it live. Before his coming old times were
a vague shadow-land, through which flitted the pale phantoms
of forgotten generations. In his novels the sun came out, and
the mists rolled away to reveal the past as a great and significant
and ever-present reality. It rose sharp and clear in vivid pictures, and we saw, as never before, that it was our own past,
that we were ourselves in the story. We saw our ancestors
at work upon the social fabric in which we ourselves reside.
We perceived that we were successors to a family estate, and
that without a knowledge of those old times we could not
hope to understand either the institutions we possess, or how
in fact we came to be what we are.

Let us very cheerfully admit that Scott's works are full of
errors. But let us at the same time recall the story told in
Lockhart of the French sculptor, who had executed an equestrian
statue of the Czar Peter. He lectured in Rome, and comparing
his own with the ancient statue of Marcus Aurelius on the

Capitoline Hill, pointed out all the anatomical imperfections of the horse upon which the Roman emperor is seated. He then turned to his own faultless model, took a pinch of snuff and remarked, ' Nevertheless, gentlemen, it is necessary to admit that this miserable animal is alive, and that mine is dead.'

But it is time to turn homewards. Look around you anywhere in this country from the Solway to the Shetlands, from Ailsa Craig to Berwick Law, and you are reminded of the man, whose name, by a magnificent coincidence, sounds like Destiny. Scotland is, she has become, for millions over all the earth the land of Scott. I cannot recall any other author who has so identified himself with his country's scenery and story, so exemplified in his own person her peculiar sentiments and virtues. Till he arose, it is no more than the truth to say, the world knew little or nothing of Scotland. He drew all eyes to her, and made surrounding nations bow to the genius of his native land. For them he is Scotland's shining mirror, in which they see reflected her lakes and mountains, her towers and abbeys, lore and history, her strong progeny. You may go further and say that her own children knew little or nothing of their country till Scott enthroned her as a queen of Romance. So incalculably vast is our debt to him that we can scarcely begin to calculate it. Try to think of Scotland without him. How impoverished ! Who among her sons and daughters has brought her the greatest honour ? It is Scott. The greatest love and admiration ? Again, it is Scott. The greatest wealth ? Well, the most materially minded of Scotsmen—if indeed there are any materially minded Scotsmen, who adhere to the gold standard—must admit that this Romantic has put money in their purses, and is to be reckoned among their commercial assets. Truly did Leslie Stephen say, ' the old town of Edinburgh should tremble to its foundations if a sacrilegious hand were laid upon his glory.'

There is a peculiarity of genius that has hitherto, as far as I know, been overlooked. Great men have a knack of choosing the right moment to be born. As in Homer the shining Immortals descended from Olympus to take part in the battles of the Greeks and Trojans, so from some coign of vantage on the ramparts of eternity these great men perceive an opportunity in the plains of time and descend to our assistance. Scott chose his moment well. Edinburgh, it has been truly said, then ' monopolized pretty nearly all the philosophy which existed in the island, and a great deal of the history and criticism.' His arrival secured for her a splendid supremacy over all rivals. Is there any reason why our Scottish nationalists should not aim at a restoration of that supremacy ? Or is there any other aim which would so greatly have rejoiced Sir Walter's heart ?

I have used superlatives, but I was wrong to employ them, for a cold catalogue of his services, not to this country alone, but to humanity, would suffice. And of such services we are at all times in need. There is no escape from the conclusion that life has always been and will remain hard. The world is no paradise, and we but deceive ourselves if we dream of a sovereign remedy for its pains and distresses. It is the high privilege of the poet and artist amid these inevitable accompaniments of existence to provide fair visions for our refreshment, to bring us some measure of support and consolation, to be the sword and buckler of the human soul on its strange and dark adventure. Happy is the man to whom Heaven has granted the privilege so to help his fellow-creatures. And never did Heaven, I think, confer a greater blessing on this country than in the gift of Scott.

' I glory in the thought,' said Maria Edgeworth, ' that my name will go down to posterity as his friend.' On occasions such as this we, his friends, are met, it is supposed, to do him honour. Ah, no ! We are but honouring ourselves. What need has this man of our garlands and our praise ? What need of memorials ? His native land is itself his monument, a house of fame not easily shaken.

Thomas Campbell

That ours is an age of Science, I suppose no one will be found to deny; an age conspicuous above all others for its discovery and invention; an age in which, though we ourselves belong to it, we hardly know whether to admire most the breathless rapidity of its progress, the genius of its investigators, or the variety and magnitude of their achievements. Our minds to-day are filled with the conceptions of Science, our lives directed by her counsels, our language saturated with her phraseology. So dazzling have been her victories that we have eyes for no others. Nor is it surprising, for there is something Olympian in her air. Miracles are her stock in trade. She raises her hand and averts a pestilence. Her voice travels upon the ether as fast and far as ever did Jupiter's. Her thunderbolts are comparable to his own. By her imposing, and to us common mortals unintelligible and almost divine, mathematical and physical devices she surprises the secrets of creation hidden in the remotest star, or in the constitution of the very elements themselves. These are not rhetorical expressions. I make no apology for them. They are simple statements of plain and positive fact. Viewed singly these triumphs of science in our time delight us; viewed as a whole they may well stagger the imagination.

What have literature and the arts in the present or in the past generation to set over against all this? What comparable achievements? Respectable and interesting they have been, no doubt, even brilliant, if you will. But what names of poets or of painters can we oppose in generous rivalry to those of Darwin or Kelvin, of Clerk Maxwell, or Pasteur, or Lister —to name but a few among the leaders of thought—in their influence upon the course of the world or the ways and lives of men ? I will not venture for their own sakes to recall any, for few would sustain the comparison.

But turn back a page or two of history, and how changed the landscape. When Thomas Campbell, a hundred years ago, delivered his address as Lord Rector of this University, who were then the men of light and leading ? Byron, unexampled in renown, was just dead, Scott at the height of his fame. Crabbe and Moore, Wordsworth and Coleridge, Keats and Shelley, poets all, had been for long the names on every lip. Abroad, Goethe and Heine, Hegel and Schopenhauer, Leopardi and Victor Hugo swayed the thought of Europe. Poetry was then in the ascendant, and poems were something more than poems. They ranked as public events. The poet was a personage, a man of consequence in the body politic. Can we say that he is so any longer ? In ancient days, we are told, a quotation from a poet—Homer—was sufficient to solve a political problem. But in ours it would not serve, I fear, to settle even a municipal dispute.

Poetry has receded from her pride of place : we hear no longer of the ' sacred bard.' The interest and attention she once aroused are gone. They have been usurped by the new knowledge, its masters and exponents. Not wholly, let us hope, nor for ever. Prose and reason may suffice some of the children of this age, but we cannot forget that the background of human life remains, and must remain, the same. History, too, suggests that when the interest in poetry goes, it does not go alone. When she is in eclipse vital elements in the moral atmosphere are withdrawn. For she appears to be the priestess in the temple of the spirit, who tends the sacred fire, and trims the lamps of piety and patriotism ; keeping alive the ancient loyalties, which are the cement of human society, the love of beauty, too, and hope itself—that singular flame in us which sustains all our private and collective efforts, and without which the whole fabric of our existence would crumble into instant and irretrievable ruin.

In 1777, the year of Campbell's birth, the Humanities were still the inspiration of ardent youth, and here, in Glasgow, both at the High School and in the College, they remained without a rival in his boyish, as in after life in his maturer, affections. Seven cities, it is said, contended for the honour of Homer's birthplace. No city but Glasgow can claim a hair of this poet's head. He was a Campbell on both sides of the house. He was educated at a Glasgow school and in Glasgow College. I should add that he was baptized by the Professor of Moral Philosophy in Glasgow ! What more could Fortune do for him ? He seized his opportunities. While still under fourteen he took prizes in Latin, and, like Pope,

'Lisped in numbers, for the numbers came.'

In attendance on the classes here he distinguished himself, not only by his verse translations of Aeschylus and Aristophanes, but at seventeen—they were giants in those days—by a prize poem upon no less terrific a subject than *The Origin of Evil*, which gave him celebrity, we are told, and well it might, 'throughout Glasgow, from the High Church down to the Salt Market.' Metaphysics have never in Scotland, as in England, been confined within University walls, and Glasgow was at that time, the poet himself tells us, 'a city flowing with syllogisms and ale.' The opinion of the Salt Market in the matter of poetry was not to be despised, for within three years the verdict of its critics was the verdict of the country. If this be the winter of their discontent, it was then high summer for the poets. *The Pleasures of Hope* secured for its young author, at twenty-one, immediate recognition. It opened for him the doors of the literary circles, brought him the acquaintance of Henry Mackenzie, 'the Man of Feeling'; of Dugald Stewart and Archibald Alison, celebrated philosophers, both of whom had studied in Glasgow before him ; and, best of all, the friendship of that most noble soul and glorious genius, 'the great and gallant Scott,' enthroned at Edinburgh in the love and admiration, not of Scotland only, but of the world.

Unlike many poets, resentful of all restrictions, civic or collegiate, who have little to say in praise of their universities or their teachers, Campbell never spoke of either save in terms of warm affection. From the first a lover of the old learning, he remained throughout life an enthusiastic Grecian, reading while at College not merely the ancient authors, but all that the German commentators had to say about them. To such terrible, to such fantastic lengths may a poet be carried by his enthusiasms ! Steering his course by the polestar of the classics, his Greek, as he said, ' his pride and solace at every period of his life,' he seemed more anxious to be considered a scholar than a poet, and delighted in every opportunity to display his learning. ' I have been talking Latin so long,' he wrote from abroad in 1820, ' that I have hardly sufficient English to tell you of my arrival in Vienna.' The love of Greek is an intelligible passion, but we cannot acquit the poet of a certain unreasonableness when he complains of his Irish charwoman—Irish, not Scottish—that she had no knowledge either of that language or of Latin. Parnassus and Helicon filled all his thoughts. During one of his vacations he roamed Argyllshire with a friend, ' feeling a soul in every muscle of his body,' and the lads ' sang and recited poetry through the long, wild Highland glens.'—' Your letter was far too full of love,' he wrote to a correspondent. ' A poet should have no mistress but his Muse. What smile of a virgin is so bewitching as the smile of Calliope ? . . . What august beauty so dignified as Melpomene ? ' These are very proper sentiments at eighteen, but he was married at twenty-six. In the year 1800, with a poetic reputation already established, he embarked at Leith on a literary pilgrimage to Germany, his eyes bent on Jena and Weimar. At Jena, Fichte was lecturing, to be followed in 1801 by Hegel ; at Weimar, Goethe and Schiller, the twin stars of German poetry, were shining in full strength. But other and more threatening lights were in the sky. The long war between France and Austria broke out anew, and impeded the traveller, who found himself entangled in its tides. So closely, indeed, that he witnessed a charge of dragoons, and near Ratisbon drove across a battlefield, where the bodies of men and horses still lay upon the blood-stained ground. 'This formed,' he wrote, 'the most important epoch of my life in point of impressions ; but these impressions at seeing numbers of men strewn dead on the field—or what was worse—seeing them in the act of dying, are so horrible to my memory that I study to banish them.' It was with these experiences in mind that he wrote *Hohenlinden*. A year later, on his return home, Campbell found himself, as a result of some curious error, under suspicion of treason. His papers were seized and examined, but the only treason found among the manuscripts was a copy of *The Mariners of England*.

From 1803, when he was twenty-five, Campbell saw little of his native town till he returned as Lord Rector in 1827. London offered brighter literary prospects than either Edinburgh or Glasgow, and the young poet had learnt the terrors of an empty purse. Marriage, as dangerous an undertaking as poetry itself, increased those terrors, and he exclaims, ' Adversity, take any other shape than poverty ! ' borrows fifty guineas from Scott, and turns, like many another poet, before his day and since, to lectures and journalism, of less engaging features, but often better paymasters than the lovelier Muses. Soon, however, his friends rallied round him, and a Government pension of £200 a year relieved his anxieties.

The career of a poet or man of science rarely offers exciting material to his biographer. Their thoughts may shake the world, but as citizens they commonly pass peaceful and un-eventful lives. Shakespeare, to our displeasure, aroused little curiosity in his generation ; Newton and Darwin created no flutter in fashionable society. Nothing sensational can be nar-rated of Campbell. ' The world has been very indulgent to me,' he said, and it is true that he early gained and never lost the esteem of his contemporaries. Among the celebrities of his day he moved on equal terms. Abroad he met Humboldt and Schlegel; in England he made the acquaintance of Fox and Wellington, Grattan and Brougham, Byron and Sydney Smith, Crabbe and Moore, Rogers and Washington Irving, Madame d'Arblay and Mrs. Siddons. To us it is of interest that he knew James Watt, the engineer, who owed to this University the encouragement and assistance which enabled him to complete his great invention. There is no need to go further. He was an accepted poet. As a man he was warm-hearted, modest, disinclined to censure, generous in praise of talent, a lover of children. Such a man could not lack friends; he deserved them.

We need not as I have said, expect from a poet activity in the world of affairs. So far, indeed, from expecting it, I suppose most of his neighbours regard him as a probably harmless, but certainly superfluous person in the body politic; or at best, to employ Bishop Creighton's witticism, no doubt ' as good as gold, and fit for heaven, but of no earthly use.' Putting aside for a moment his poetical value, Campbell has at least one claim upon the consideration of the practical man. It is to him that the University of London owes its existence. The idea took shape in his mind during a second visit to Germany, whose Universities played so large a part and exercised so wide an influence in the national life. The cost of an education at Oxford or Cambridge—then the only Universities in England—and the Church tests imposed upon candidates for their degrees, restricted in that country the advantages of higher education to the privileged few. To widen the opportunities of the many, and offer a career to able and ambitious youth, irrespective of their financial resources or religious convictions, seemed to him an imperative public duty. The time was ripe and the proposal welcome. The University was established; to be followed in the succeeding generations by the provincial Universities, which are now beginning to do for England what ours have done in Scotland for close on five hundred years. He was proud of this successful excursion into the public arena. Various titles were at different periods of his life conferred upon Campbell by his admirers. In his youth he was called *The Pope of Glasgow* ; his advocacy of the Polish cause in 1832 brought him the designation of *the Poet of Freedom*, but he asked for himself ' no better epitaph than to have been one of the promoters of a University for London.' A modest claim, surely, for a poet. But if this was, in his own judgment, his most important work, ' the crowning honour of his life ' was the Lord Rectorship of this University, to which he was elected in 1826 by a great majority. I am loath to mention it, but I fear most of the Professors supported the statesman Canning. So immense, however, was his popularity with the students—' a sunburst of popular favour,' as he called it—that he was re-elected in 1827, and again in 1828 : a rare distinction. In his address, Campbell, speaking of his old College, made use of the phrase, ' the genius of the place itself.' It is a happy phrase. For in ancient universities, as in old and famous cities, in venerable churches, in scenes enriched by the passage of great events, wherever moving chapters of human history have been written, there lingers, there resides the spirit of departed days, *the genius of the place itself*, a pervading and compelling presence, a source of inspiration and of power.

Still other honours awaited him. In 1836 Campbell once more revisited his native country. ' It would savour of vanity,' he wrote, ' to tell you how I have been received. Cheered on coming aboard the steam-boats—into public rooms—cheered on leaving them.' And again, ' I have been made a freeman of Edinburgh, and fêted like a prince.' He suffered one disappointment indeed ; the burgesses of Paisley refused him the freedom of their city. But he bore it bravely, and declared on his return to London that the three months he had just spent in Scotland were ' the happiest of his life.' It was not his last visit to the North. But the poet's health was failing. He had lost many of his Scottish friends, and the old happiness was never to be recaptured. In search of health he visited Wiesbaden, and in 1843 took a house at Boulogne, ' to educate my niece,' he wrote, ' at a moderate expense, and to live, upon the whole, more cheaply.' There, in June of the year 1844, he died, and a week later was buried in Poet's Corner, Westminster Abbey ; near the spot where, at the funeral of Garrick, Dr. Johnson had stood and wept sixty-five years before.

Among Glasgow poets Thomas Campbell is by far the most famous. Alone of those educated in this College he attained national eminence. He lives still, nor is it likely he will ever cease to live. Let us ask, not was he worthy the honours which fell to his lot in life, but is he deserving of that far greater honour, not readily to be yielded, a seat among the immortals ?

It seems, if we ponder it, a strange thing, and to many men will always remain a mystery, why a mere verbal dexterity, or what appears to them a mere verbal dexterity, should be so highly valued, why a few lines of verse, a dozen or two maybe, should suffice to carry their author's name, when vast multitudes are wholly forgotten, safely down the stream of time, and secure for it everlasting remembrance. So the world, however, has decreed, and the present is not the hour to question its decrees. Let us allow that Campbell has obtained from that incorruptible jury, posterity, a verdict in his favour, that his fame is secure. Let us ask only, is it justified ? We know that he was a harsh judge of his own compositions, never satisfied ; that he often discarded what had cost him weary hours to produce. We know, too, that he had ever before his eyes ' the pure lines of an Ionian horizon,' the standard set by the masters of Greek literature. To have always in mind the highest kind of excellence is a great thing in any art. To be yourself the severest critic of your work is a second great thing. To despise easy success is a third. Campbell wrote comparatively little. It was not, I think, that, as Scott suggested 'he feared the shadow of his own reputation.' It was rather that he had a close acquaintance with the noblest literature of the past, and that his mind and hand were checked by it. He had a fear of the world's best, and there can be no more wholesome type of alarm. How desirable if to-day we could convert it into a widespread panic ! In general the works whose value is known only to their authors and concealed from their readers are composed without reference to such a standard, never submitted to comparison with the great classics. Browning says somewhere :

> 'Aeschylus' bronze-throat, eagle-bark for blood
> Has somewhat spoilt my taste for twitterings.'

Campbell's taste, formed in the select society of the best, protected him against twitterings, and against the dreadful facility which betrays so many writers. It was wholly in his favour that his education had burnt into his mind the knowledge that 'all excellent things are as difficult as they are rare.' Campbell never, even in youth, sowed wild oats in his verse. No one, indeed, could in a fever of enthusiasm describe him as faultless. I do not refer to his scientific inaccuracies. In some of his longer poems—*The Pleasures of Hope* and *Gertrude of Wyoming* —he strews them lavishly. He introduces tigers to the shores of Lake Erie, hyænas into South America, and panthers into Ohio. Flamingoes, aloes and palm trees find themselves where, it appears—I should never myself have discovered it—Nature never placed them. These, and errors such as these, may perhaps be regarded as covered by a poet's licence. They occur, however, in poems with which we need not occupy ourselves. Time has settled their account. He said all he had to say in them, but unfortunately had nothing to say. They are not without their felicities, their catching phrases, once much admired. Who has not heard of 'angel's visits, few and far between,' or quoted

> ' 'Tis distance lends enchantment to the view ' ?

Fine things, you maintain. Yes, but these fine things cannot save them. As poems their day is done. They are out of sight and clean forgotten. We must look elsewhere for Campbell's claims to immortality. What remains? A handful of lyrics, a few hundred lines of verse. Too slender a foundation, it might be argued, for an enduring monument. In this matter, however, it is never quantity but always quality which tells, and quality alone. Sappho's is an imperishable name, yet how few are the stanzas that preserve it. And many of our own poets, the most familiar, like Gray, were far from prolific. There are even single poems the world will not willingly let die. A song like Jane Elliot's *The Flowers of the Forest* or Graham's *If Doughty Deeds My Lady Please* may keep an author's memory alive for a thousand years. Let us set about writing them! More than that, the poet's talent, as we know, often gives to persons and places and things a value which is without any justification save a poetical justification. The honey of Hymettus is not the best honey, even in Greece, but the poets have talked it into fame. The fight at Roncesvalles was a mere skirmish, but the *Song of Roland* exalts it to a place among the greatest battles of the world. This talent, this power appears to rest upon a universal human passion, in a word the passion for beauty. With the shapely things, the lovely things, whether the poet's, or the musician's, or the painter's, our affections are linked in some mysterious union. They alone possess the *elixir vitæ*, and outlast the short-lived generations of men. As Wilkie, the painter, stood in the Escurial, gazing at Titian's picture of *The Last Supper*, an aged monk said to him:

'I have sat daily in sight of that picture for nearly three score years; during that time my companions have dropped off, one after another; more than one generation has passed away, and there the figures in that picture have remained unchanged. I look at them until I sometimes think that they are the realities, and we are but the shadows.'

A handful of lyrics, then, will suffice—they have often sufficed to defy the blotting finger of time—to make their author's name a household word. And if we examine the collection of our lyrical poetry which has been accepted as the best, if we examine the *Golden Treasury*, the little book so familiar to all of us, we shall find, perhaps to our surprise, that Campbell occupies as large a place there as Gray or Scott, nearly as large a place as Keats or Burns themselves, poets whose names are writ in marble, in more lasting material than marble, in the hearts of their countrymen. It may be answered, ' Yes, but he is without inwardness, the things of the deepest significance in human life he leaves untouched.' The same criticism was directed by Carlyle against Scott. But can there be a greater folly than to depreciate a talent because it is not another talent, or to ask from a man more than he has to give ? Certainly it was not in Campbell's power, it was not in his nature to attempt a justification of the ways of God to man, to deal with the larger hopes and fears, the profounder thoughts and experiences of our strange and uneasy existence. Again, we hear that he was a rhetorician rather than a poet. But I distrust the categories of the critics. I recall the old debate, ' Was Virgil an orator or a poet ? ' Virgil ! ' The chastest poet and the royalest that to the memory of man is known.' Distinctions, indeed, we may and must draw, and admit that the grand subjects, the grand style were beyond Campbell, that it was not within his province to add :

' The light that never was on sea or land.'

He knew it well enough, and spoke with depreciation of his own ' drum and trumpet lines,' as if they were of small account. But patriotic and heroic poetry are not to be so lightly dismissed. ' Certainly I must confess my own barbarousness ' ; said Sir Philip Sidney, ' I never heard the old song of Percy and Douglas that I found not my heart moved more than with a trumpet.' Such poetry is not to be dismissed till love of country, till delight in heroes and the heroic perish out of the world, and of such calamities we need have no fear. Campbell, it may also be urged, dealt only with simple and customary themes. I cannot think it a grievous fault. For what is literature after all but the books people like to read ? And what is enduring literature but the books generation after generation continues to read ? And how simple they are. How simple is all great art. The glittering summits of obscurity are easy to attain. Show me unintelligible poetry and I will show you poetry that may be praised by superior persons, but is never read. There is nothing more difficult, as Horace knew, than to make a commonplace your own, to put into the mouths of your countrymen the words they cannot find for themselves, the very words they desire to use. Campbell found those words, not once but often, and it is his glory. It is, perhaps his peculiar glory that he wrote the only martial lyrics in our language that have gained universal currency—*The Mariners of England* and *The Battle of the Baltic*. It has been said of England, and by an English poet :

'Thy story, thy glory,
The very fame of thee,
It rose not, it grows not,
It comes not, save by sea.'

The sea, inconstant to others, has been her constant ally, her nursing mother and guardian ; her sailors are her greatest pride. Yet it was left to a Scottish poet to write the poetry no Englishman had written, of the sea and English sailors ; to celebrate Nelson, the best-beloved, almost worshipped hero of the navy and the nation. An achievement surely most surprising and most enviable.

That is not, however, Campbell's sole achievement. In that inimitable ballad *Lord Ullin's Daughter*, or, better still, in *Hohenlinden*—to take a single example of his lucid and admirable art—we have verses of which any poet, whatever his rank, might with pride have claimed the authorship, which ' not even a god, though he worked hard,' could easily improve. How many poets in our day, and we have them in plenty, have produced anything so perfect in its kind ? How immediately it arrests the attention, how economical the phrasing, how vivid the language, how complete the picture it presents ! Such is its art that the difficulties overcome are not apparent. It appears an easy thing. Not until we approach a like undertaking do we appreciate its accomplishment. Then its truly formidable character reveals itself ; then, and hardly till then, do we realize that poetry worthy the name is so difficult as to be well-nigh impossible. You think that statement an exaggeration ? Well, take up again the book to which I have already made reference—*The Golden Treasury of English Lyrics*. It is, let me remind you, the harvest of more than three hundred years, the harvest of our whole literary history from the sixteenth to the present century ; the history, too, of a people by the world's consent illustrious in poetry, so illustrious that no other people can with confidence be placed above it. Yet how slender is the book in which the lyrical verse, the golden grain of those centuries is garnered. During those centuries a legion of poets has been at work, and has added—if you will permit me a curious calculation—has added, the whole choir of our poets in session—how much shall we say ? At most forty or fifty lines annually to the national treasury. That is the consummation of all their lyrical labours, all their toil. For the rest, it may have pleased their contemporaries, it pleases no longer. So unwilling is Fame to confer an unfading laurel. A depressing thought, perhaps ; yet in that book, slender as it is, Campbell has his not inconsiderable sheaf. And if some critics in these days think but poorly of him, there are others whom we may regard as at least of equal authority, Goethe and Byron and Scott, who were of a contrary opinion. We are far too inclined to suppose that our estimate, the judgment of our own day, is the last word on a writer, that ours is the casting vote which determines finally his position

M

in the hierarchy of letters. It is a mere arrogance. I sometimes wonder what the judgment of our predecessors, of Milton or of Wordsworth, would be upon the poetry of to-day, or what will be the verdict of later years upon the works and judgments of the present. I wonder and tremble. Campbell, however, is not dependent upon the suffrages of this generation. He has already taken his place at the table with the makers of our literature. Those among them who were acquainted with his writings received him into their company, and that is enough.

In classical times, at the oracle of Delphi, a strange and signal honour was, we are told, accorded to the poet Pindar, the ' Theban eagle,' the lyrist, of unequalled splendour, who praised in song the athletes and heroes of his country. At the offering of the sacrifice the priest proclaimed aloud that the god himself desired the society of the poet's shade. We dare not, indeed, compare our poet with so far-shining a genius as Pindar, but may we not claim that he had Pindar's love of eminence and conspicuous achievements, and something at least of his authentic fire? And may we not also, in the name of Apollo, patron of the arts, echo the ancient words, and say, ' Let Campbell, the poet, come in to supper with the god ' ?

Tolstoy [1]

We are here this evening to do honour not to a man of our own race, nor even to a lover of it, neither to praise patriotism nor patriotic service to the state. We meet for a less usual purpose, to place in public view the portrait of a writer who has neither national nor municipal claims upon our attention, who had little or no sympathy with our political or social systems, no admiration for our country's history and no respect for its heroes, who detested our ideals and in his later life laboured to belittle the greatest of our intellectual representatives, Shakespeare, the pride of all English-speaking peoples. And in so doing we may, perhaps, take to ourselves some degree of satisfaction that we can escape at times from the contemplation of our own affairs and our own provincial perfections into the larger and salutary area of interests wholly human.

It would indeed be surprising if a voice so full and vibrant, so moving and pathetic as that of Leo Tolstoy had left us cold and unresponsive. Born though he was in a country remote and unfamiliar to most of us, the child of traditions strangely foreign to our own, we in this little island, itself the cradle of a great empire, could hardly fail to recognize in that voice something of the significance and power of the vastness of Russia, something prophetic of its yet unfulfilled and incalculable destiny. And the man, apart from the author, how arresting is the story of his life, a life one might say agitated by every emotion, every experience within the range of our natures.

Born in 1828, thirty-three years before the liberation of the serfs, Count Tolstoy belonged to the land-owning aristocracy

[1] At the unveiling of a bust of Tolstoy in the Municipal Art Gallery, Glasgow.

of his country. Nothing, it seems, in his appearance suggested birth or breeding. Shy and awkward as a boy, plain to ugliness —for long a source of bitter distress to him—' I imagined,' he said, ' that there could be no happiness on earth for a man with so broad a nose, such thick lips and such small eyes as mine.' As a young man of fashion, as a university student, as a soldier, his pursuits were those of his class, and he was distinguished from his companions only by his love of reading, and particularly by the fits of repentance and resolutions of reform which followed his indulgences. ' He came back from his Sebastopol battery,' said his friend Turgenief, ' put up here and is going the pace. Sprees, gipsy girls and cards all night long—and then he sleeps like a corpse till two in the afternoon. At first I tried to put the brake on, but now I've given him up, and let him do as he likes.' Already a thinker, his habits tormented him. The cup of pleasure was embittered by a sense of sin such as haunted Bunyan in his unregenerate days. For some years after his marriage in 1862, during which he wrote *War and Peace*—the oasis of his life—the sky cleared, his restless spirit ceased to prey upon itself. But the clouds gathered and the horizon soon darkened again, and whether he looked within at the condition of his own soul or without upon the wretched estate of his fellow-countrymen, misery took hold on him. From his earliest to his latest years his mind remained the battlefield of conflicting emotions. At one time, while serving in the Crimea, thanking God that he had lived in that glorious time, a few months later declaring war inhuman and indefensible. Fired at one stage of his career by the perfections of Greek literature he proclaimed that ' without knowledge of Greek there is no education,' and determined ' never again to write wordy rubbish.' At another later stage he could find no better words to describe the Greeks than that they were ' a small, semi-savage, slave-holding people, who lived two thousand years ago, imitated the nude human body extremely well and erected buildings pleasant to look at.'

Never at rest, dissatisfied with his position as a land-owner, his profession as a soldier, his habits, his art, even his family life ; harassed by religious doubts, by moral doubts, eternally vexed by the desolation and misery of the peasant millions of Russia, by every problem, spiritual, economic, social that rears itself against the heart and mind, by that Hydra, that many-headed monster, which in our self-conscious age tortures the sensitive conscience, he sought refuge finally in an interpretation of Christianity which rejected the whole structure of modern civilization, condemned art and culture, denounced states and statecraft, laws and law-courts, private property, the use of money—proclaimed the doctrine of absolute non-resistance to evil. It brought him no peace. ' He has become a Christian,' wrote his wife, ' and is quieter and more depressed.' Unhappy in his intellectual, he was no happier in his domestic life, and driven by the same merciless demon of unrest spent his last hours and breathed his last breath in a self-imposed exile from his wife and family, from whom he fled as if from a brood of pursuing furies.

At long intervals there are born into the world men who find for their private wrongs or personal sorrows an audience wide as earth itself. Of such was Byron, who, as Arnold reminds us—

> ' Bore . . .
> Through Europe to the Ætolian shore
> The Pageant of his bleeding heart—
> Till thousands counted every groan,
> And Europe made *his* woe her own.'

At long intervals, too, there are born into the world men who seem to take upon themselves the whole burden of suffering humanity. Never perhaps in human history has any one man before Tolstoy so suffered, as it were, in his own person, the wrongs of the world, and at the same time gained for his personal sorrows and conflicts of soul so universal a sympathy.

We see him bent, like a storm-tossed tree, before the tempest of human wretchedness ; we see him, too, confiding, like a child, his private afflictions to all who would hear them, to receive both as sufferer and sympathizer the amazed attention of the civilized world. Like Byron, who, despite his frailties had in him so deep-seated a humanity that his cry of pain caught the hearts of his hearers like the cry of a child, Tolstoy, too, had the child's sublime egoism. So evident was his suffering, so convincing the utterance that announced it, none could pass indifferently by. And as Byron's poetry is an autobiography so are Tolstoy's writings, from the first line to the last, the expression of personal and passionate experiences. By another road than Shakespeare's, who escapes us while we, even in our innermost thoughts and feelings cannot escape him, Tolstoy, whose soul lies open to our gaze, reaches the centre. And how is it reached ? With the same pen and at the same moment he writes of himself and of us. It is the way of genius. What is common to all forms of genius is sensitiveness. How alive are the artists to impressions that escape or half escape most men. The musician, the painter, the poet builds each his house of thought from materials, colours, tones, words, familiar to all, within anyone's reach, but to whose values he is more immediately responsive. Tolstoy was not, indeed, a poet, but he had ' the devouring eye and the pourtraying hand ' ascribed to Carlyle by Emerson, he was a great writer. Had he been a poet we could hardly have judged of his greatness save through a knowledge of Russian, the language in which he wrote, for it is by his execution, his expression that the poet is known, and in translation one can hardly judge of it. But that he was a great writer is clear to us, his possession of ' those thirsty eyes, those portait-eating, portrait-painting eyes ' of which Emerson spoke. The vividness, the intensity, even in translation, of his pictures of life are a sufficient proof. No reader of his best novels, *War and Peace* and *Anna Karenina* will deny it. Great artist or not, and we may set aside that question, his characters are at least no wooden puppets, they think and feel and move and speak as convincingly as the men and women we daily meet and know, they are magnificently alive. Think of Anna, think of Wronsky, think of Levine, of Sonya and Natasha. Unmatched in his own generation, though we bring against him the novelists of every country in Europe, Tolstoy's men and women look out from his canvas like the portraits of the great masters. We know they are authentic. That is his first claim upon us, and it is a commanding claim. In praising Tolstoy's creative work we are celebrating a victory of the human mind which falls short, indeed, of such a triumph as Dante's or of our own Shakespeare, which falls short of the highest because it is not a poetic triumph, by far the rarest and most difficult to achieve, but is still an intellectual victory of which not Russia only but the human race itself may well be proud, and must for long preserve in grateful memory. Yet in later years Tolstoy himself came to despise it. After his so-called conversion the current of his life was changed. 'What formerly used to appear good in my eyes appeared evil,' he tells us, 'that which used to appear evil appeared good.' Deliberately he cast aside his divine talent. 'Art is a lie,' he wrote, 'and I can no longer love a beautiful lie.' He abandoned the ideals of the artist that he might enter a wholly different region, the region of religion and morals, there to ask himself, 'What am I and what am I to teach?' And here in this new sphere of activity, in this field where the battles of the mind have raged most fiercely, if universal acceptance be denied him, he found at least an audience of no less eager and sympathetic listeners. Nor need it surprise us. When a man proclaims that after long and anxious enquiry he has at length found the secret of true happiness, the precious philosopher's stone for which the whole world is ever in search, when a man proclaims that he has found it, especially if he be a man of Tolstoy's genius, who is not ready to lend an ear?

There are critics, indeed, who dismiss, and not unnaturally dismiss Tolstoy's claims to a hearing in the field of religion and morals on the ground that in practice he was a poor disciple of his own theory, on the ground that he was inconsistent and ate freely of all the forbidden fruits. Natural as the objection is, we may, I think, set it aside as irrelevant. Or we may answer it in his own honest and pathetic words, ' If I know the road home, and go along it drunk, staggering from side to side, does that make the road along which I go a wrong one ? ' That he had found the road home Tolstoy believed with sincerity, that he could indeed point out to the human race, so long a wanderer in the wilderness, the way to happiness. Let us accept it or not, the vast, disruptive, far-reaching scheme he proposes to us, let us call him a true or false guide, one thing is easily recognized, that we have in him a representative man, that in a very living sense the present age speaks through him. For if it be anything ours is a questioning age, and Tolstoy questions everything—our education, our art, our social life, the dogmas of our religion, the very foundations of the State. He lays the axe at the root of our civilization. For England and the English his is a hard doctrine. For we are a practical rather than a speculative people and suspicious of theories and abstractions. The greatest of our political philosophers, Burke, a name never to be mentioned without reverence, had a horror of the doctrinaire, of the metaphysician let loose among the institutions of society. He believed in the slowly accumulated and capitalized experience of mankind, that there and there only wisdom lay. He held that our social and political institu-tions represented the best that had been known and thought by the community that created them, that, built up by generation after generation, they represented the peculiar genius and answered to the circumstances and needs of the race. ' What,' he asks, in one of those weighty sentences of his, ' would become of the world if the practice of all moral duties and the founda-tions of society rested upon having their reasons made clear to every individual ? ' One might well shrink from so gigantic an undertaking. Yet though so cautious and practical a people as ourselves may well hesitate to destroy the ship in which our ancestors have made so long and successful a voyage, and to accept Tolstoy's solution of our doubts and remedy for our ills, the grim and ugly and sordid features of our materialistic civilization become more grim and ugly and sordid when the prophet's accusing finger is pointed at them. If he makes us uneasy he is justified by the uneasiness he causes. Like Rousseau, of whom he was the ardent disciple, Tolstoy—and herein lies the secret of his strength—turned from the satisfied contemplation of the gilded apex of the pyramid of society, the art and culture and leisured luxury, to a dissatisfied contemplation of its base, the slavery and wretchedness, the poverty and ignorance and squalor in which it is planted, upon which its foundations are laid. To approve of this passion for the welfare of the majority is not difficult, and we are all willing enough to share it. More, too, than in Rousseau's day the majority has found its voice, and is not easily to be silenced. But we must not overlook what Tolstoy overlooked, that there is happiness as well as misery in the world. He forgot that there is such a thing as happiness even when life is hard. Goethe speaks somewhere of Lazaretto poetry, of poets who write as if the whole world were a hospital, a Lazaretto, and contrasts with theirs the Tyrtaean poetry which ' not only sings war songs but also arms men with courage to undergo the conflicts of life.' There is in Tolstoy much of the Lazaretto, less of the Tyrtaean strain, and his least discriminating friends must regret it. But they will answer our criticism by pointing to sentences like the following—' I cannot seek a culture which separates me from men. I cannot refrain from seeking in my whole existence—in my lodging, my food, my clothing and my ways of going on with people—whatever, far from separating me from the mass of mankind, draws me nearer to them.' In our reflective moods, and with an eye upon the infinite diversities of men in race, in religion, in circumstances, in aspirations, we may set aside his ideal as impossible or unintelligent, yet the generous impulse, the anxiety for human welfare which every-where meets us in Tolstoy, the strain of feeling which animates such words must win all hearts.

In these days when West and East face each other as never before in the history of the world, when, as we are commonly told, Asia has awakened under the touch of Europe, it is not altogether an idle speculation whether we can count upon the victory of the West, whether we can assure ourselves that the ideals of Europe will finally triumph. It may prove, indeed, that Asia will, as often before, give more than she takes, that remaining indifferent to our views of life she may impose on us her own. Asia dropped the plummet into the deepest waters of speculation while Europe was still a continent of barbarians. From the East came our religion, our philosophies, from the East all the arts of civilization. And once again, it seems, through the mind of this great writer, comes to us the voice of the East, calling us to a new and difficult way of life. For, as a recent biographer tells us, and tells us truly, we shall not understand Tolstoy until we recognize the Asiatic in him, and the denial of life that is at the root of all the Asiatic religions and philosophies. Listen to that voice and one seems to hear the accents of some Buddhist sage persuading us to turn our backs upon the pursuits and pleasures, the frets and fevers of the world to seek the path, the upward heavenly way. ' One cannot deceive oneself,' he writes in his *Confessions*, at the age of fifty, ' it is all vanity. Happy is he who has not been born. Death is better than life, and one must free oneself from life.' Hear him as he describes his ' unceasing ecstasy ' over Schopen-hauer, that ' occidental Buddhist,' that protagonist of despair. ' Schopenhauer,' he cries, ' is the greatest genius among men.' Hear again his view of women—' We must regard the society of women as a necessary unpleasantness of social life, and keep away from them as much as possible.' And after his conversion what has he to say? 'The Christian ideal is not marriage: there is no such thing as Christian marriage. Marriage from the point of view of a Christian is not an element of progress, but is a fall. Love and whatever precedes it and follows it is an obstacle to the true human ideal.' And if we ask of his conversion itself, to what was he converted? We must answer, not to Christianity, for there is no Christian dogma he is prepared to accept. 'I have no predilection whatever for Christianity,' are his words. 'For me the doctrine of Jesus is simply one of those beautiful doctrines we have received from Egyptian, Jewish, Hindoo, Chinese and Greek antiquity.' Nor does his creed include even a belief in immortality, that pivot of the faith, the hope not of Christians only since the birth of mind. To what then was he converted? To a belief, it seems, that existence is an evil, and that the wise man is he who extinguishes desire, and with desire the will to live. He cannot be said to have added anything to that ancient doctrine, preached more than two thousand years ago on the banks of the Ganges. Is Europe proof against this doctrine, and if not, what are we to hope for, what are we to expect?

Tolstoy, then, believed that he had found the only pathway to happiness; it lay through asceticism. And a great love and pity for mankind consumed him, as it had consumed Prince Siddartha so many ages ago in Benares, love and pity for his fellow-men, lost in the wood of error, beset by the illusions of time. Some earnest seekers after truth will no doubt accept the hard doctrine, and will ask Europe to accept it also. Others will turn back from the later to the earlier Tolstoy, to the artist who was lost in the prophet. And some will, perhaps, sigh like Goethe, when in his old age he looked round him upon young Germany, for 'less philosophy and more power of action.' And thinking of Tolstoy sitting in sackcloth and ashes, without courage or hope, casting away from him all that life has to offer, the question rises to our lips: 'Is this the report we must give to the younger generation, the children, the newcomers on the stage of time?' What a message for them on the outset of the journey! 'Happy is he who has not been born.' And perhaps Englishmen may ask themselves whether, pagan as was its authorship, their own *Beowulf*, with all its melancholy, has not in its steadfast strain, its sense of duty done and of happiness in leading even a forlorn hope, a better word to say, as had, too, Bunyan's pilgrim in the dungeon of Giant Despair. For to the question 'Why should ye choose life seeing it is attended with so much bitterness?' he answers, 'I am resolved to pluck up the heart of a man, and do my utmost to get from under his hand. Let us not be our own murderers.' At least if we are true to the traditions of our race we shall look around us for weapons and resolve to die fighting. And we shall continue to believe that the world has need of a hero of the old English or of the Greek pattern, a cheerful Hercules, undertaking mighty labours for mankind, rather than of a creed which is a condemnation of history, of all that men have wrought to make earth orderly and friendly and habitable. And to be afraid of music and poetry, to be afraid of the love of the sexes, to be afraid of beauty, how strange are these fears! Some of us when we think of this dread of sex and art and beauty will recall philosophers who met life without any such alarm in a spirit of courage and largeness and liberality. Some of us will prefer Plato when he argues for another method of proceeding towards the doctrine of love—

'beginning,' as he says, 'from these beautiful objects here below ever to be going up higher with that other beauty in view; using them as steps of a ladder; mounting from the love of one fair person to the love of two, and from the love of two to the love of all; and from the love of beautiful persons to the love of beautiful employments; and from the love of beautiful employments to the love of beautiful kinds of knowledge; till he passes from degrees of knowledge to that knowledge which is the knowledge of nothing else save the absolute Beauty itself, and knows it at length as in itself it really is.'

Some of us will continue to prefer Plato, yet we shall none the less willingly remember that Tolstoy was a great lover of the people, and that he was a giant, a Titan.

Thoughts for the Times

Here we are in the year of Grace, 1940—the year of Grace !—
and the sirens wail their dismal warnings over our country day
and night, while 'the airy navies grapple in the central blue.'
Thoughts which move to such accompaniments can hardly fail
to be coloured by them, and it was not long until I laid aside
the subject upon which I had at first intended to address you
for a very different one.

'This is not a time for jesting,' said Voltaire in 1765, 'wit
does not harmonize with massacres.' We must, I think, agree
with him, and add for ourselves that the discussion here to-day
of some literary or æsthetic question, otherwise appropriate
enough on such an occasion, would not harmonize with the
thunders and lightnings of war, would, indeed, be singularly
out of tune with the thoughts that in the present hour assail
and possess our minds. If that be your feeling, as it is mine,
I may, perhaps, better meet your wishes by turning away from
academic themes to deeper and more fundamental matters,
which are never out-moded, since they occupy the centre
and are increasingly the subject of mankind's most earnest
consideration.

Needless it is for me to describe the days in which we live,
for we are in the midst of them, days throbbing with the anguish
of a tortured world. Exalted issues, issues of an infinite consequence are in fierce debate. Never in the world's history have
greater been in the balance, never have the passions of men
been more deeply stirred. And around the scene of fateful
action are ranged as in a theatre a vast concourse, a thronging
multitude of spectators, awaiting with strained and breathless
attention the outcome of the stupendous conflict. They are
gathered as to a great assize. For not only are their own fortunes, the fortunes of millions at stake, not only are the destinies

of unborn generations in the balance—indeed the whole future of the human race—but, whether they are conscious of it or not, the innermost character, the intrinsic qualities of men and nations over all the earth are displayed, and on fiery trial. Doomsday is here. Now, if never before, they have made a revelation of themselves, and are known for what they are. The mask has fallen from the features of combatants and non-combatants alike. All the pretences, pretexts, concealments, hypocrisies by which peoples are accustomed to deceive their neighbours, deceive no longer, and are become transparent glass. Everywhere the nations have, however unwittingly, made full self-confession, and pronounced a final and un-challengeable judgment upon their own sense of values, their own worth, their own natures.

At this assize some have declared themselves neutrals. They deceive no one. For when, as in the present hour, all human rights are in deadly peril, when the bully stalks abroad, the assassin strikes down his victim, there are in effect no neutrals.

In this affair you are for freedom or against it, for justice or against it, for humanity and decency, or against them. And in the choice you make it is yourself you judge.

I believe, then, you perceive, that never throughout its long past has human nature made such a pitiless exposure of its infirmities, so clean a breast of its baser self. The philanthropists, jealous for the good name of the species, will very probably labour in excuses, yet, even for the most determined among them, it has been anything but a comforting or cheering spectacle. They will look long and far to discover grandeur, generosity, nobility among the peoples, warring or at peace. Without doubt many magnificent, many noble and heroic episodes have been inscribed upon the record, but against what a miserable background of falsehoods and treacheries, desertions, disloyalties, cruelties, perjuries, betrayals, so that we seem to stand at the gates of hell, where, in Schopenhauer's phrase, ' men are the demons,' not in the vestibule of evil, but at the very headquarters of Satan himself, the enemy of mankind.

When the volcanic forces we see at work, the long-imprisoned fires of the underworld exploded, it was with unexpected and terrifying violence, and took by surprise the civilized peoples, unprepared for the ordeal. Yet the eruption was no bolt from the blue. For not to speak of the last war, it had been preceded by signs and portents, premonitory rumblings, and should by any intelligent observer have been foreseen. Manifestly, throughout Europe, and, indeed, over all the inhabited lands both in the East and West, an ominous restlessness had long prevailed. The links which bind societies together had been for generations in process of dissolution, and who could fail to perceive a disintegration of the entire framework of Christian civilization ? To the careless passer-by it presented an imposing façade enough, its towers still stood proudly against the sky, but its unseen foundations were in decay. Of all the age-long beliefs, customs, traditions, of which the venerable structure was composed, not one had escaped the enfeeblement of age, and the sapping inundations of the great tides of advancing science. No dykes, no barriers, sufficed to arrest their destructive course. Everywhere, on all sides, the marks of a decaying order, of changing fashions of thought, were to the discerning eye clearly visible, and time itself seemed in sympathy with, and in respect of them, to march to a new and double-quick rhythm. We have witnessed a social earthquake, a vast disruption of human thought. The spirit of a restless enquiry had for a century, or longer, been in the saddle, taking nothing for granted, sparing no creed however sacred, no institution however revered or successful. Under an avalanche of destructive criticism the whole fabric of society trembled, and the rising generation entered into possession of a melancholy inheritance— the crumbling faiths and moribund loyalties of its forefathers. Adding knowledge to knowledge and flushed by its victories the unrelenting inquest continued. 'Let us see for ourselves with our own eyes,' cried the exultant intellect, echoing the words of Voltaire in his first tragedy, ' let us be our own oracles and tripods and gods.' That a custom, a belief, a convention belonged to the old tradition was enough. That fact alone consigned it to the limbo of contempt. Western civilization appeared bent on suicide. No society can with impunity break away from its past, no single generation can build a state or nation. What but anarchy and confusion can be looked for when a people cuts itself adrift from all that its forebears have thought, and believed, and loved, to embark without chart or rudder upon the wide ocean of speculation ? If, in any society, the bond between the living and the dead be not preserved, corruption and decay are the inevitable sequel.

' Let us be our own oracles and tripods and gods.'—What havoc this mad, however heroic, resolve has wrought with the fundamental articles of the ancient faiths ! A deadly dialectic loosened and undermined human confidence in all the codes and conventions, the rules of life implicit in the existing constitution of society. Every argument, it was presently discovered, met its match in a contrary argument of equal force, until in the mellay nothing appeared capable either of proof or disproof. How in such a wild and whirling world could human relations in any solid or ordered form be preserved or sustained ? To know what to do you must first know what to think, and what was one to think ? Do I exaggerate ? Tell me, then, of any firm ground in science, in politics, in economics, in religion, in morals upon which I can stand in security, or lay the first stone for an enduring home of thought. Show me a conclusion in physics, in biology, a theological tenet, an ethical principle, a law of life not called in question, upon which doubt has not been cast. Have I, perhaps, in the surest of the sure sciences, in mathematics a safe retreat ? ' Mathematics,' announces Mr. Bertrand Russell, in a famous epigram, ' Mathematics may be defined as the subject in which we never know what we are

N

talking about, nor whether what we are saying is true.' Can I believe in the venerable maxim that parallel lines cannot meet, or that Euclid, master in the province of the most rigid demonstration known to man, said the last word on geometry ? By no means. In the geometry of Riemann the supposed impossibility takes place, and as for Euclid, ' It is nothing short of a scandal '—again I quote Mr. Russell—' that Euclid should still be taught to boys in England.' Can I confidently suppose that every event must have a cause ? I should be sadly out of date were I to make any such antiquated assumption. Have I never heard of Hume's criticism of causality, or Heisenberg's Uncertainty Principle ? Was it religion in which we put our trust ? Worse and worse. Surely there is no one in these enlightened times so ignorant as to be unaware that religion in any form whatever has, by the leaders of modern opinion, been finally set aside as nothing more than ' the whimsies of monkeys in human shape ' ? ' Philosophy removes from religion,' announces Croce, ' all reason for existing.' Can I take shelter within the last defence of the old order, the moral law, the central keep of the social system ? Again disillusion awaits me. Hume, long ago, echoing Spinoza, made the categorical statement, now almost an accepted commonplace, ' Morality is determined merely by sentiment,' and Nietzsche cast Christian ethics on the rubbish heap as the contemptible babble of slaves. Our old familiar world, how we cannot tell, has fallen around us in ruins, and we shall never see it or know it any more. Condemned on all sides, yes, yet how like a star it shines beside the present !

' The advent of cannon,' said Napoleon, ' killed the feudal system ; ink will kill the modern social organization.' He also is to be numbered among the prophets. Very well, then, let us now look around for the new wisdom, the new and better principles which the rationalistic critics, the wise men who were to be ' their own oracles and tripods and gods,' proposed to substitute for the old and discarded articles of the earlier doctrine, their suggestions for the guidance, government, protection and welfare of the great European communities.

The site had been cleared, the demolition was complete. But now arose a difficulty. The architects of the new order found themselves, in Huxley's phrase, ' standing on a point of nothing in an abyss of nothing '—a somewhat unpromising situation. Once again the gods had placed the pretentious, posturing manikin, the human intellect, in its place. In such circumstances it is not a matter for astonishment that the building of the New Jerusalem has been indefinitely postponed. You will, I think, seek long and vainly even for so much as the ground plan of the Palace of peace, justice, plenty and happiness which in the good days at hand was to house the European family. Nor should we be astonished that in such a season of bewilderment an opportunity offered itself, an opportunity perhaps the most favourable in the whole history of mankind, was provided and seized by the powers of darkness to declare war upon a confused and defenceless humanity. A more propitious day for the great assault upon its most precious and dearly won possessions, upon justice, freedom, goodness, decency surely never dawned. It was not of course so described, but set forth in roseate terms— after the manner of all devices of the pit—as the establishment of a new and better order. When the consciences of men are confused, their convictions unsettled, their minds clouded and distracted, their defences are down. It is then that they clutch at straws, it is then that they are in the greatest peril. The hour of the garrison's perplexity is the hour of the besieger's opportunity.

I suggest to you that the most noble and potent of human instruments, the intellect, has one, but in respect of the concerns of society, a fatal weakness. It destroys faster than it can build. Moreover, it does not, and in its very nature is unable to, provide the cement that holds communities together.

The forces which make for unity, for social cohesion, are not to be found in the understanding—a stranger in the recesses of the soul. It overlooks, since it cannot comprehend, the affections and passions. It never, for example, speaks of those mysterious influences, those mighty factors in the human story, the love of home and the love of country. Reason separates men, they argue, they disagree, they quarrel. Speak to them of what they love, their horses, their dogs, their gardens and hobbies, and you win their sympathy. Feelings in common, common hopes, loves, fears, a common way of life, in a word a communion of souls, to which the intellect makes no contribution, these are the mortar of societies. To overlook the part and the slow part played by the affections in the unification of human communities is, then, an error of the first magnitude. If the mechanical side of life, if utilitarian pursuits, if science and scientific views usurp and monopolize our interests, if the intellectual or rationalistic prevail over the simple human elements in our lives, the heart hardens, the spirit droops. Romance, poetry, gladness, fade out of existence, and with the drooping of the spirit, the hardening of the heart, all hope of social and political cohesion vanishes utterly away. ' Science without conscience,' said Rabelais, ' is the ruin of the soul.' To that pregnant utterance we may add a saying by an acute · thinker a generation ago, ' the fatal flaw in this emotionless culture is that it contains no sort of human amalgam strong enough to hold society together.' If then we as a people stand alone and successfully in the present crisis of our fate, it will only be by the revival of the deep-seated affections, of the hidden elements in the nation's heart, which, to the confusion and astonishment of our foes, have sprung again to life in our country's and the world's defence.

I have not suggested, and am far from suggesting that we are ourselves wholly responsible for the calamities which have befallen us. Nor can all our troubles be laid at the door of the politicians. We cannot, indeed, crown them with garlands either for their luckless activities or inactivities—one is at a loss which to admire least—but they were not supermen, and forces beyond the control of mortals were at work. None the less, let us be honest and confess our shortcomings. As a nation we were unsuspecting, for which there is some excuse. We were blind, for which there is none. It was a wilful blindness. You may plead that the errors of judgment in our estimates of the character, designs and resources of our present enemies were not moral but intellectual errors, and by contrast, pardonable. But was it so? Did those mistaken estimates not spring from negligence, carelessness or disinclination to face the facts? And are these not moral delinquencies? Between moral and intellectual errors the Greeks, clearsighted here as always, were slow to distinguish. From the charge at least of grave contributory negligence, I fear we cannot as a people be excused. What may have been creditable to our hearts was extremely discreditable to our wits. Yet there is another, and the major factor in the evil case. How came it, how can we account for it, that Germany, a country many of us knew in our youth as harmless enough, not at any time, perhaps, celebrated for the elegance of its manners, or the sobriety of its pretensions, yet not wholly without science, art or letters, how came this country to accept the domination and direction of its present rulers, a reptile crew, if ever there was one?

I use plain words for plain things. They will be, I think, the words of posterity. Or if not, if this judgment be not endorsed by future generations, is it conceivable that the human race will acclaim these rulers as good men and true, as friends of humanity, and their doings as patterns of behaviour for imitation by statesmen in the days to come? If these men be then worshipped, as undeniably they are at this hour worshipped by admiring millions, of what clay will their worshippers be made? Explain it how you will, it is not to be denied that the chief of the European dictators has become the German god. Judge then of the race which bows the knee to this animal, this self-confessed liar, as its chosen deity, to be served with fanatical devotion. It is composed of his accomplices in actions I do not say unworthy of civilized men, but of a tribe of cannibals.

For we can no longer nurse illusions. We have witnessed a revelation of the German soul in all its nauseating brutishness. A sorry sight, indeed. Not long since there was much talk of Versailles. Germany posed as 'the injured innocent.' We were then told that it was to Versailles we should trace the miseries which have overtaken Europe. We are to believe, then, that the subsequent robbery and destruction of the Jews, the political assassinations in Austria, in Germany itself, the execution or murder of some 70,000 Poles, 24,000 of them women and children, the unprovoked invasions of inoffensive lands, of Denmark and Norway, the fiendish massacre of the innocents in Rotterdam, 30,000 of them within an hour, quiet citizens of a friendly state, the deliberate slaughter of fugitive peasants on the roads of Belgium and France—all these proceedings are to be attributed to Versailles. Versailles has, indeed, something to answer for. It would not be surprising if those who went about with this lunatic lie upon their lips were to declare Versailles responsible for the Fall of Man, or the Flood in the days of Noah. By others, who cannot bring themselves to admit any unpleasant truth, except to the discredit of their own country, German behaviour is to be ascribed to social or economic grievances, or German need for *Lebensraum*. They have short memories. Before 1914 Germany was a considerable colonial power. She was admirably placed for the conquest of the world's markets. The ball of an unexampled commercial prosperity was at her very feet. None the less these advantages did not restrain her from a wanton and unprovoked attack upon Belgium. No. However coaxed by our 'pacifists' and pacificators, those miserable birds refuse to fly, and we can no longer deceive ourselves, be deceived or nurse infantile illusions. It is nothing short of a revelation we have witnessed, an undisguised outpouring of the German soul, a soul, it would seem, incapable of shame or ruth, rejoicing in hypocrisy and deceit, proudly parading the features no longer of men but of snarling wolves. Nothing comes from nothing ; what is not there cannot be revealed. You cannot fill yourself a cup of wine from a muddy well. It will take more than appeasement, more than economic arrangements, a good deal more, to transform Germany into a neighbourly and friendly associate, a country which to accomplish her hateful ends stabbed her honour dead.

To rid this piratical people of the passion to enslave or destroy weaker nations is clearly beyond ours or any human power ; what may be possible is to deprive her of the weapons by which to pursue such aims. Before exchanging compliments and commodities with a wild beast it would be a wise precaution first to draw its teeth. For we have—it is no mere nightmare—strayed into the pages of a picaresque novel, a type once in vogue, which had its humours, in which all social virtues and values are reversed, in which brigands are the heroes and pickpurses the men of mark. What was accounted in ordinary human life as blameworthy has become praiseworthy. The assembled and admiring company in the thieves' kitchen is the scum and riffraff, the scourings of the underworld, and has a code of its own, the code of the parasites of society. Thimble-riggers are the admired of all beholders, gangsters and gallows-birds in armoured cars assume the airs of statesmen. In fiction all very amusing no doubt, but somewhat less entertaining when the action has been transferred to the high stage of history, the history of our own times. The incredible has happened. The cruel ogres, the giants and dragons, of our childhood's story books have come to life. Nevertheless the frightfulness by which we are appalled is no novelty, no sudden and pardonable outbreak of madness. Its baleful star appeared in the campaign of 1914, and was then advertised and defended. It is a calculated policy, a deliberate, meditated, organized infamy. To Germany belongs the credit, the exclusive, the proud privilege, of its invention as a method of warfare. Hers is the word, the thought and the thing, hers, and for ever, the unenvied crown of savagery.

She, too, was the inventress of totalitarian war. Where other peoples have desired to mitigate its accompanying horrors, her thoughts did not run that way. They soared to higher heights—the all-inclusive slaughter of men, women and children, the more comprehensive the better.

Many years ago, when lecturing to my class here on Marlowe, I quoted a passage from his drama, 'Tamburlaine.' In that play Babylon is captured and Tamburlaine orders that its citizens, bound hand and foot, be thrown into the city's lake. He is asked what is to be done with their wives and children, and answers :

> 'Drown them all, man, woman and child,
> Leave not a Babylonian in the town.'

The good lads in my audience were vastly amused by this outburst. It was too preposterous. Such things did not happen. Only in the fevered brains of lunatic poets did such monsters exist. They know better now, those boys. After Rotterdam, Darwin's thesis needs no further demonstration. Those who ordered and executed that piece of work had not reached the level of human beings. They were beasts, brute beasts.

If there be no redeeming features in this picture let us put the matter to the test, and ask for one such feature. Will anyone tell us of a single magnanimous act, a single generous gesture, a single inspiring sentiment, a single charitable proposal, a single courteous rejoinder amid the furious discharge of threats, the medley of abuse, boasting, insults, vituperation, not even 'wittily wicked,' which, mingled with fantastic nonsense, characterizes the public utterances of Nazi spokesmen, the cataracts of vulgarity with which they flooded and fouled the world ?

I am not so foolish as to declare or believe that Germany contains no sane or decent folk, who hate and deplore the Hitler régime. I am prepared to think them numerous. Let us also make the handsome admission that we are not ourselves to a man or woman either saints or angels. Nevertheless if, as its history, past and present, abundantly demonstrates, the German nation is subject to periodical fits of homicidal mania, it is no safe neighbour, and a strait waistcoat becomes the only possible treatment of the recurrent malady. We are not speaking here of imaginary things, but of actual events never to be overlooked or forgotten, burned into our souls, gigantic horrors on a gigantic scale, nations on the rack, and the crucifixion of Europe, of which we have been ourselves the startled spectators. The facts speak for themselves.

It was said of Nero by a Latin writer that his purpose was 'to uproot virtue itself'—*exscindere virtutem ipsam*. And if to eradicate virtue itself, to renounce humanity, to bring upon the planet more desolating wretchedness than any one man had ever succeeded in inflicting upon his fellow-creatures, if this were the ambition of the most conspicuous of the European dictators —he, I mean, the professed connoisseur in guile, who prefers the colossal, or German style in the architecture of deceit, the gigantic lie—if this man's ambition were to adopt as his motto 'Evil be thou my Good,' and remain loyal to it, if this were his aim, it can hardly be denied that it has been magnificently, after his own manner, successful. Since Hitler hoisted the skull and crossbones, the black Pirate flag, the former princes among the world's criminals might well, were they alive, tremble for their laurels.

The modern dictator is in no need of military, or any other genius, unless perhaps it be a genius for dirty work, including assassination. 'Is there any cause in nature,' asked Lear, on the dark night of his anguish, 'Is there any cause in nature that makes these hard hearts?' And we, centuries later, may make a similar unanswerable enquiry. Is there any cause in the heavens or in the earth why whole nations should turn upon themselves, and take measures for their own degradation? And yet, as do most human circumstances, the situation exhibits a certain wry humour. While here in Britain our well-meaning thinkers, seated in their book-surrounded studies, were busily engaged in the construction of ethical theories, something not unimportant escaped their attention, nothing less, indeed, than that the greater part of the European world had ceased to be at all, or in any way, interested in such matters. These brilliant men, absorbed in their academic meditations, failed to observe that they were living in an age which had jettisoned all rules of conduct, an epoch, which, unlike any other in history, was marked by the complete disappearance of ethics as of religion, an epoch of which the wholesale destruction of London churches, of Coventry's Cathedral, and the high altar of St. Paul's, provides the most appropriate symbol. Look around modern Europe, and ask yourself, What is the most striking of its present-day characteristics? Only one answer is possible. It is simply that Europe has discarded morals, done away, in effect, with all moral considerations whatever. Their sun has set. For religious and moral principles it has substituted the simple ' Do as you please ' maxim, wherever possible, in all the circumstances of life. Nothing is more manifest, more conspicuous in these days than the utter disregard for any kind of decency in national relations or human behaviour. The air reeks with treacheries and betrayals. Treaties are not made to be honoured, nor promises to be kept. The most sacred pledge given to a neighbouring country, that its independence will be strictly respected, is recognized as the premonitory signal of an imminent invasion. Self-interest is openly assumed and proclaimed as the only sensible rule of conduct. No one in continental Europe now dreams of making the ridiculous enquiry, ' Is this right or wrong ' ? No one entertains the slightest respect for humanity, for justice or truth. Chivalry, honesty, honour—these are empty sounds, expunged from the vocabulary of the modern world, and no longer in use.

For a people like ours this complete disappearance of religion and ethics, not merely from the thoughts and actions of statesmen and politicians, but from the life of civilized nations, pro-

duces a kind of mental dizziness, a sense of unreality and stupe-
faction. For it is a people profoundly conscious not only that
religion provides spiritual power : Δεινὸς ὃς θεοὺς σέβει—
' Terrible is the man who reveres the gods '—but a people
profoundly persuaded that save upon the foundation of some
kind of religion and morals no civilization can be built, no
system of law and order established, that without them mankind
must speedily relapse into the pit, from which it has so painfully,
with such desperate exertions through the long centuries, been
digged.

I have put the query, a query not to be smilingly asked or
discussed, how is this eruption, this emergence from the underworld of the ape and the tiger to be accounted for. There is,
however, another and not less pertinent and melancholy enquiry
to be made. What sort of respect can its victims retain for
themselves, what shred of it, or what kind of excuse or apology
can they offer, that they failed to perceive or prepare for the
gathering tempest ? What sort of intelligence can they claim,
outwitted as they were by a gang of vulgar criminals, gulled
by deceits the most palpable extending over years, by falsehoods
the most transparent ? The author of ' Hudibras ' was no doubt
right when he wrote :

> ' Mankind is naturally averse
> From all the truth it sees and hears,
> But swallows nonsense, and a lie,
> With greediness and gluttony.'

Equally true it is that for its indolence or folly a people must
pay the price, often a terrible one. Yet one would suppose
that the first duty of civilization, or of a civilized nation, was to
look to its defences, to man its walls against its barbarian neighbours. For if events of this present order are at all times lying
in wait for peaceful peoples, if the vast apparatus of their
machinery, if their educational systems, if their forms of government afford no warning and provide no kind of protection

against the assaults of cutthroats, equipped with the destructive
devices of science, sallying forth to slay and pillage as they will,
one foresees strange things to come. If civilization be such a
fragile plant, if we cannot do better than we have done, Heaven
help us ! It is very possible for a man or a people to play the
fool once too often, and at this very moment far from certain
that we have not already done so.

Close upon two hundred years ago the very peril by which
we are at this moment assailed—a peril no one who has experienced it will readily forget—was foreseen in striking fashion
by one of our own writers. Listen to these sentences :

' If men were all virtuous,' says a character in *Rasselas*,
' I should with great alacrity teach them all to fly. But what
would be the security of the good, if the bad could at pleasure
invade them from the sky ? Against an army sailing through
the clouds, neither walls, nor mountains, nor seas could afford
any security. A flight of northern savages might hover in
the wind, and light at once with irresistible violence upon
the capital of a fruitful region that was rolling under them.'

Thus wrote that most sagacious of men, Dr. Johnson. ' A
flight of northern savages might hover in the wind ! '—I think
he must have been inspired. And if, as I have said, civilization
cannot or will not provide for its own preservation, if vast
barbarian hordes can be harnessed to scientific machinery and
hurled upon unoffending peoples, we are led to exceedingly
sombre reflections upon the future of the race. We have to
face the prospect of an era in which whole nations may become
the willing or helpless instruments of some half-dozen ruffians,
employed by them as mere slaves in designs far removed from
their own personal interests, under the command of taskmasters
as careless of their lives and indifferent to their welfare as were
the Egyptian Pharaohs of the serfs who built the Pyramids.
A fine tale, truly, to tell of modern man, the proud heir of all
the ages, that his use and end and destiny is to be harnessed to
the chariot of some mad dictator, or to become the miserable

dupe of unscrupulous adventurers, to be exploited, plundered, stampeded, enslaved by a handful of conspirators, a mere pawn or counter in the game of their vile ambitions. A fine tale to tell of modern man, a brilliant conclusion to our Christian civilization. When the peoples no longer control their governments, but their governments exploit their peoples, we must cease to talk of the rights of man, that fantastic dream.

In the last generation one of our novelists, George Meredith, made use of the phrase, ' More brain, O Lord, more brain ! ' Yes, we are most assuredly and desperately in need of brain. If it be, indeed, beyond the wit of man to shield himself against such assaults upon his very existence, if our schools and universities, our sciences and philosophies, provide no armour against such unfathomable ills, what are we to think of them, or how flatter ourselves upon our stores of knowledge, our vast array of institutions and organizations, our intelligence and our labours ? Flatter ourselves, did I say ? There seems little room for congratulations to ourselves that we have continued to think of everything except the one thing needful—how to preserve what we had already gained. For there it is, staring fixedly at us, that fact, that terrible oversight, which has brought us to the brink of ruin. How pitiful is man's estate, in which nothing is more pitiful than the defencelessness of the good. Goodness, in its very nature unsuspicious, affords the most tempting opportunities to malicious and unscrupulous designs. The virtuous and friendly man, honest, trusting, unsuspecting, lays bare his breast to sudden aggression and subtle cunning. He cannot by reason of his very goodness so much as conceive the malicious designs, the monstrous thoughts inhuman hearts may harbour. He cannot believe that devils exist, because devilishness is for him unbelievable. Nevertheless, nothing is more certain than the existence of devils, legions of them, in human shape. The benevolent man, too often, thinks others as benevolent as himself—a noble but how fallacious a fancy ! He thinks no evil, and is the more exposed to its assaults. He believes—kind, simple soul, all honour to him—that the right must triumph, however weighty the forces arrayed against it, that justice must necessarily prevail. But is it so? Is not the whole earth patently and palpably the scene of horrifying injustice? Does not history on its every page teach that lesson, and the Christian Bible also? We but live in a fool's paradise when we overlook, as do so many of our 'Pacifists' and Christians, the most glaring facts. Has it ever occurred to you that a man may be a very good Christian and a very great fool, that he may have a Gargantuan appetite for balderdash, or that his follies may bring more misery into the world than his Christianity brings happiness? Has it ever occurred to you that his Christianity alone will not save the missionary from the tiger, whether in animal or human shape? Nor should it be overlooked that just as there are thieves and murderers, there are predatory peoples, professional looters and man-killing races in the world. There are cannibal and robber tribes, land pirates and sea pirates, land rats and water rats. 'A criminal state is not a new thing in history.' The murder of the virtuous for no cause other than their virtue is no new thing. It is as old as the human race itself. It dates back to the murder of Abel by Cain. The extermination of innocents in tens of thousands with every circumstance of calculated cruelty forms in these very days part of Germany's deliberate policy.

History provides, I fear, sadly insufficient evidence for the doctrine that right is at all times armed with invincible might. On the contrary, let us confess the ineluctable truth that men and nations who pursue the left-hand path have much in their favour. Let society withdraw its police, its protective measures, and you will soon be convinced of that simple truth. The career of the wicked by no means invariably leads to the scaffold, or even to torturing self-reproach. There are plenty of murderers in the world, including Nazis, who enjoy easy consciences. 'I rather suspect,' wrote Plato in the *Republic*,

' that injustice, which murders others, keeps the murderer alive, aye, and unsleeping too.' In a mind intent upon evil a watchfulness, an alertness, a dreadful cunning are engendered. Such a mind is all alive, it secures and keeps the initiative. It astounds and appals by the ruthlessness, unexpectedness and violence of its onslaught. This, in my judgment, is one of the most formidable, perhaps the most formidable, of all truths. While the rest of mankind, and most especially in our own country, advanced to a greater regard and tenderness for the weak and helpless, Germany, seizing the advantage thus offered her, took the opposite path, contempt for them ; and we know the result.

It is time this chapter in the annals of mankind should be closed, and that right quickly. The new must open with the clear conviction that there are men, thousands of them, capable of any enormity, who, in the absence of resolute resistance, will stop at nothing. Over all the inhabited lands there are men willing for a price to betray their country. There are even in this land of ours men, who, under the cloak of benevolence and humanity or of Christian principles, are willing to clasp the hands of bloodstained assassins, make terms with wickedness itself and put an end to strife by striking a bargain with Beelzebub, men who would sit down at a conference table with Satan. They practise a viler and more insidious form of treachery, since they would betray the most sacred of all causes, the hopes and the future of mankind. To live without a soul to call your own, is not a Briton's idea of life. When Britain drew the sword against Nazi Germany she threw away the scabbard. It is war to the death. If Nazism survive, the Britain that the world has known must assuredly die, and the long Arctic night descend upon mankind. We may be confident, I trust, that she will not die, though to perish in the cause for which she stands were a glorious end to her island story. She will not die, nor will she share out spheres of influence with miscreants or negotiate with the lords of hell.

'Time and its ally, Dark Disarmament,
   Have compassed me about,
Have massed their armies, and on battle bent,
   My forces put to rout ;
But though I fight alone, and fall and die,
   Talk terms of Peace ?   Not I.

'They've shot my flag to ribbons, but in rents
   It floats above the height :
Their ensign shall not crown my battlements
   While I can stand and fight :
I fling defiance at them as I cry
   "Capitulate ?   Not I." '

'One is either a German or a Christian,' announced Hitler.
By some accident once in a way he deviates into the realm of
truth.   'Christ was great, but Adolph Hitler is greater,' proclaims a disciple of the new Messiah.   You cannot come to the
end of this blasphemous buffoonery.   Not only do these, our
adversaries, 'drink up iniquity like water,' in the phrase of
Keats, spill the blood of their own kinsfolk as unsparingly as
that of their foes, not only do they assassinate their inconvenient
accomplices, keep an army of spies at work in their own and
every other country and teach their children to spy upon their
families and neighbours, not only do they sow corruption before
them in the lands they invade, they employ an incomparable
skill in a congenial art, a novel, and if that can be, a more hideous
form of war which engulfs whole populations.   To onslaught
upon the bodies of men they have added an assault upon their
souls.   'Violence for the body, lies for the soul' is their recipe
for victory.   A grisly terror, a lying propaganda descends upon
friend and foe like a poisonous miasma.   A torrential mendacity,
a blinding, suffocating tempest of falsehoods, deceits, confusions,
doubts, so fill the air that men are bedevilled out of their senses.
Words are wrested out of all meaning, and language has become
a device to stun and bewilder the mind, to undermine reason
itself, with none ' to ask

    Which way the nearest coast of darkness lies
    Bordering on light.'

We are introduced to a new form of truth, truth 'made in Germany,' an *ersatz* variety. There is German 'protection,' another spelling for an old thing—'enslavement.' There is Roman valour, a form proudly eminent, displayed in the heroic destruction of defenceless aborigines by poison gas. It was held by Sir Thomas Browne that vices in one age remain vices in another, and that is was best to 'live by old Ethicks, and the classical rules of honesty.' The German Minister of Justice has set up a new ethic. 'Right,' he has announced, 'is what is in the interests of the German folk ; wrong is what harms it.' Kant has been superseded in his own country by a higher authority.

'Forgive your enemies' is a Christian and a noble injunction. But the time seems to have come for a deeper enquiry into its implications. For it is one thing to forgive your personal enemies, and quite another to forgive the enemies of goodness itself, of justice itself, of the human race itself, to forgive those who would shatter the lamps by which through a murky world its feet have been guided. I am not so sure that our public duty calls us to so hard a task.

For myself, when I hear, for example, of the mass murders in Rotterdam, or of the murder of a shipload of innocent children on the high seas, forgiveness is not in my heart, nor shall I make any effort to plant it there. If my soul be thereby imperilled, imperilled let it be. 'There is an unredeemable element in the world,' there have been deeds beyond pardon done in it, and men 'who well-nigh wormed all traces of God's finger out of them.' Charity, forgiveness, are no doubt cardinal virtues. Yet in such a world as ours justice comes first, and before all the rest. For on the foundation of justice alone can the others be built. Look after justice, and you have done well, very well. Look after justice, and on the day of its establishment many other and many excellent things will be added unto you. 'What would

o

you say,' asked a disciple of Confucius, ' about the idea that injury should be recompensed by kindness, that you should return good for evil ? '—' If you returned kindness for injury, and good for evil,' he replied, ' what would you return for kindness, and what for good ? No ! Recompense injury and evil with justice ! Recompense kindness with kindness, good with good.'—' He who loves his enemies hates his friends.' By all means then, let justice be done to our foes, but in our anxiety that the murderer be not too harshly treated let us not altogether forget his victims. Their claims rank first. Let us at least see to it that wherever possible reparation be made to the lands Germany has wantonly mangled, the folk whose wives and children she has massacred, into whose lives she has brought misery and desolation unspeakable.

Nazi Germany would have us believe their country inhabited by a fair, blue-eyed, Nordic race, excelling all others in every noble quality, whose destiny it is to rule the world. It seems on the historical evidence a more arguable proposition, as I have heard it argued, that ours would be a happier planet were this unique people, compact of all the virtues, wholly to perish out of it. Germany, the originator of five great and recent wars, has lighted the fires of a consuming hate in many devastated lands, and daily adds fuel to their flames, the flames of righteous hate—hatred of the cold, ferocious, deliberate, diabolical cruelty she claims and preaches as her own peculiar gospel. With the obtuseness which is her curse, she knows not what she does. When the winds of adverse fortune blow upon her, as blow they must, she will know and feel the raging heat of the fire she has kindled, and, cowering in horror, find no escape from its merciless fury. Let me quote to you the words of a Delphic oracle to the people of Sybaris :

' You have not shrunk from incurring the vengeance of the gods. To those who have wrought evil, the accomplishment of justice is not to be postponed or stopped by prayers, not even if they were the offspring of Zeus. But upon their own heads and upon their children it rolls and woe mounts on woe in their halls.'

Many and eminent philosophers inform us that the distinctions drawn by human beings between good and evil, justice and injustice, are with God of no account. These words signify man-made prejudices or preferences, matters of taste, to which nothing beyond the narrow human horizon corresponds in the wide universe of being beyond and above us. 'God's will and reason,' in the celebrated words of Spinoza, 'have as little in common with ours as the Dogstar has with the dog, the barking animal.' And again, 'The terms good and bad indicate no positive quality in things regarded by themselves, but are merely ways of thinking.' In the sight of God, that is to say, there is nothing either good or bad, right or wrong. He is high above such trivial considerations. Spinoza speaks very frequently and very confidently about God, and in this opinion he has the enthusiastic support of Nazi Germany, which, in its haste to resemble God, has also abolished these distinctions.

I cannot claim for myself Spinoza's insight into the Almighty's mind. It is not to me as to him an open book, and I must stand in reverence before any human intelligence so assured and so profound. Yet if such be God's nature, this only I will say : ' Away with such complacent deities. We can do better for ourselves without them, find better ways of spending our time than in their worship, thoughts, though human, better suited to our condition, and ideals worthier of our resolute attachment.'

During my adventures among the metaphysicians I have come upon many strange doctrines, among others the very interesting notion that evil is nothing positive, a mere negation or absence of good. Even St. Augustine comforted himself with this pleasing reflection. Personally, I find in it little encouragement. I go further. I venture, of course with profound respect, to pronounce its adherents mad. What consolation, what sense can be derived from the knowledge, if knowledge it can be called, when we look around us at the broken hearts, the bodily tortures, the mental anguish that mortals endure, that in all these there is to be discovered nothing positive ? Heavens and Earth ! I can find nothing more positive around the globe to-day. Of all devastating clap-trap, metaphysical clap-trap is the most exasperating, because it is the most pretentious. Doctrines are doctrines and philosophies are philosophies, formidable enough in their time and place, yet none so formidable and convincing in all times and places as the testimony of universal human experience, the granite rock against which the seas of all verbal juggleries burst in vain. And what has this universal human experience to say in this matter ? Something, I think, to the purpose, known to Homer, known to Dante, known to Shakespeare, known to the poets since the world began, the least deceived, the most discerning, the wisest of men,

> ' to whom
> The miseries of the world are miseries
> And will not let them rest——'

that the principle of evil, its frowning presence and strength, is, in the dispensation of mortal things no less powerful than the principle of good, if not more powerful, so powerful that many have been persuaded that good and just men are on the losing side in the encounter. Evil made early entry into this world, its days are not numbered nor its natural strength abated. For, as the strength of the maniac in his paroxysm is as the strength of ten, so evil in any of its forms gathers to itself a host of allied powers, and collects a superhuman energy, a passion and momentum to which virtue seldom attains. Injustice, as Plato has it, is ' unsleeping,' dynamic, aggressive, in its very nature the active and attacking power. Devil calls to devil, falsity hastens to the assistance of malice, hypocrisy provides armour for treachery, vanity engenders jealousy, and all stand together in a conspiring brotherhood

> ' Arm'd with Hell flames and fury.'

Against this solidarity of embattled powers what madness, what ruin to suppose that innocence is its own protector, that in this jungle world a feebler mind, a weaker resolution will, if only good intention be associated with them, suffice to carry the day. The just and good simply cannot afford to be less intelligent, less vigilant, less wide-awake than the wicked and unjust. If harmless as doves, they must be as wise as serpents. The despairing cry of ' Peace ! Peace ! ' is to the aggressor a mere symbol of weakness, and an invitation to the attack. It avails no more than non-resistance or flight from the battle. By flight a man may possibly save himself ; others, or his cause, he cannot save, and it is an argument difficult even for the casuist to sustain that in a war of principles, and clearly the present is a war of principles, either submission or running away is the highest type of human endeavour.

When I find myself at any of the famous crossroads of thought, where the darkness thickens, and decisions are hard, I retire for my encouragement upon certain convictions, fixed stars in my little firmament. Here is an instance. Whatever men elect to call them, I continue to believe that deceit remains deceit, cruelty cruelty, treachery treachery, kindness kindness, justice justice, as certainly as food is food and poison poison, and that villainy, however successful, is still villainy. Of this very old-fashioned, simple-minded conviction—let the metaphysicians say what they will—I am unable to rid myself. Here is another. When I am told that throughout the realm of nature there is no ' tendency that makes for righteousness,' that justice is nowhere to be found there, that in her soil the tree of justice refuses to take root, that search the universe from pole to pole, and save in the heart of man even its seeds will be sought in vain, I do not, on that account, admire nature the more and man the less, I do not find nature ennobled and man humiliated in her mighty presence. Quite the reverse. To me it seems to exalt him to a plane immeasurably far above hers, and moreover to provide him with an aim, a purpose, a cause, an inspiration that fires the blood and hardens resolution. If justice be no concern either of nature or of the gods, it is the more pre-eminently ours. If no claim to support justice be elsewhere advanced, let us advance it. If this world be without justice it is man's unique privilege to place it there—a superb design, an enterprise the immortals might envy, yet have left to mortal hands. ' Ah ! ' said an American visitor to London, when he was shown the Law Courts, ' Ah ! That is where you get justice, dear, but prime.' I am far from sure that it can at any time be cheaply bought, but sure I am that it is worth the price however high. And of another thing. That in the British heart there burns no passion than this for justice with a purer, inextinguishable flame. This, too, I believe, that it burns more fiercely in the British people, that they are prepared to make for it greater sacrifices than any other people in the world to-day. Fair dealing, fair play, is the idol of the British heart. It is then no accident, no freak of chance, that Britain now stands, and stands alone in its defence.

O dear and honourable, whatever may befall, O fortunate and happy Britain ! we must wonder at you, as all men wonder, the mother of a Viking brood. See them on sea and land, your sons, see the young eagles gather in the skies above your eyrie ! see, and be glad. In such an hour how must our affection for you burn with an ever brighter flame, so favoured of heaven as we are to be at your side in this the greatest day of all your greatness, to share your hopes and fears, and griefs and exulta- tions—you who, not counting the cost, threw into the scale of destiny wealth, empire, security, existence itself for the freedom which is your breath of life. How proud a part is this you play in ' Battle's Parliament,' to be the sole guardian of human rights, to be in all the world their chosen shield, the helper of peoples without a helper ; you who ' nothing common did or mean,' disclaimed no promises, deserted no ally, dealt no felon's blow, broke no faith, nor bit the kindly hand of any neighbour, any friend : you who wounded by betrayals, stricken by disasters, remained Britain still, that land the summit of whose peril is ever the summit of her glory. We must wonder at you, you whose follies are mountainous, yet whose very faults become you, so foolish you are and so wise ; we must wonder at you, dear, foolish, incomparable, angelic land, the most dangerous and most generous foe that ever drew sword among the nations. Men and poets will have, I think, whatever may betide, much to say of you in the yet far distant days, and be envious of us, who breathed the perilous air when the old lion at bay raised once again his kingly head to look around upon his adversaries, a sight to see. And as the Greek genius forged out of human sufferings and sorrows the noblest art, the art of tragedy, so may Britain build out of the wounds and terrors of the present conflict the loftiest memorial of her spirit, to be seen afar and shining through all the centuries to come.

'Not without toil to earth-born man befalls
To tread the floors of Jove's immortal halls ;
Never to him, who not by deeds has striven,
Will the bright hours roll back the gates of heaven.'